THY LOVE
AND THY GRACE

VOVS QVI LAISSES LE MONDE OYEZ MA DOVCE VOIX
DONNES MOY VOSTRE COEVR SVYVES MOY A LA CROIX

THY LOVE
AND THY GRACE

AN EIGHT DAYS' RETREAT
FOR RELIGIOUS

BY

CUTHBERT LATTEY, S.J.

B. HERDER
PUBLISHER TO THE HOLY APOSTOLIC SEE
LONDON, W. C. 1.   1923   ST. LOUIS, MO.

Imprimere licet

Londini, die 16 Martii 1922

Gulielmus Bodkin, S. J.,
Praep. Prov. Angl.

Imprimatur

Friburgi Brisgoviae, die 23 Decembris 1922

Dr. **Mutz**, Vic. Gen.

To the Greater Glory of God
and in loyal memory of our holy father
Saint Ignatius of Loyola
now, upon the tercentenary
of his canonization,
declared by the Vicar of Christ
Pope Pius XI
the heavenly Patron of all retreats
and of all institutions and associations
that promote them.

PREFACE.

THE present volume has for its sub-title, 'an eight days' retreat for religious', and is intended primarily for those who are bound by the three religious vows of poverty, chastity and obedience. The fundamental principles of a virtuous life, however, are the same for all, whatever their state of life, and it is hoped that priests generally, consecrated as are their lives to the service of God, may not find it difficult to adjust what is said to their own work and their own needs, and that even the devout laity may find the book helpful.

If the work possess any claim to originality, it would be based upon the careful (yet prayerful) study alike of the New Testament and of the Spiritual Exercises of St. Ignatius. The more the present writer has made and given retreats, the more strongly he has come to feel that as Christ is the Key to the Spiritual Exercises, so the Spiritual Exercises may reverently be called the key to Christ, the philosophy, as it were, of His life and teaching, and a powerful help for the soul towards complete surrender and abandonment to her Divine Lover. In this

way the Exercises are also a key to the great
apostle St. Paul, since none have ever set forth
so passionately and so profoundly all that the
God-man is to mean for us. Perhaps reference
may here be made to the present writer's little
book, *Back to Christ*, wherein the various pre-
sentations of the Person of Christ are considered
with something more of scientific method.

An audacious innovation is the prefixing of
some verses to the several sets of meditations
assigned to each day of the retreat. The offence,
if offence it be, is a deliberate one. We are
apt to take a somewhat prosaic view of a retreat,
whereas it should be the most chivalrous venture upon which ever knightly soul was set.
Such it was in the mind of the soldier-saint Ignatius, and for a token of his yearning we find
the *Anima Christi* at the head of his Exercises.
The first four poems appeared in the *Beaumont
Review,* and the translation of the *Caelestis Urbs*
in the *Tablet*; thanks are here offered to the
editors for leave to reproduce them. The language of poetry, and especially of such magnificent poetry as the inspired lines of the Hebrew
psalms, helps that affective movement of the
will which is so much more to be prized than
any mere perception of the understanding; for,
as St. Ignatius says, 'it is not the abundance of
knowledge that satiates and satisfies the soul,
but to feel and taste things internally'. If, there-

fore, many considerations are here offered for the understanding, such a proceeding must be interpreted according to the spirit of St. Ignatius, and of St. Paul, or again, of St. Teresa, as expounded in the seventh chapter of her Sixth Mansions. These considerations may serve in various ways to enkindle the fire, or to direct its energy; but they are not the fire itself.

Somewhat in the same spirit a frontispiece has been chosen, a photograph of a quaint old picture that hangs in the refectory of the London residence of the Society. My thanks are due to the Superior for leave to print it, and to Fr. J. H. Pollen, S. J., who has very kindly given his personal assistance in the matter, and has offered the following notes upon the picture. It is a representation of the religious life under the form of a royal lady, who though crowned lets her orb lie idle and inverted on the ground. Her whole attention is directed to the Crucifix before which she is kneeling; her hair falls free, to denote that she is unmarried, her hands are united in prayer, and a heart is resting upon them. It is in flames, and on it are written the letters representing the Holy Name, IHS (Ihesus), with a cross upon the middle letter. The figure of the Crucified is represented as suavely as possible, the wounds being very small, without sign of blood. The Cross grows out of a chalice, and immediately passes into a vine. On the

other side of the Cross are two angels, one
with a harp, the other with a mandolin. Below
runs the inscription in old French:

> Vous qui laisses le monde,
> Oyez ma douce voix;
> Donnes moy vostre cœur,
> Suyves moy a la croix.

The last letter of the word *croix* is of a debased
form. Heraldry and architecture point to the
middle of the sixteenth century as the date of
composition, and for neighbourhood to the Walloon
provinces of the Netherlands. The picture is
especially suitable as a frontispiece to a work
such as this, not only by reason of its subject,
but because in all probability it is not far removed
by origin from the time and place of Thomas
a Kempis, and may be another offshoot of the
spiritual movement which produced the Imitation
of Christ.

In conclusion, may this little venture help some
to spread abroad the good odour of Christ, in
a world so rank with immorality and unbelief.
And may they commend to God's mercy the
writer, who is not unaware that to treat of such
high matters means in a measure to be condemned out of his own mouth.

C. L.

CONTENTS.

			Page.
First	Day (Peace: God: The Light: Confession)	.	1
Second	Day (Reverence: Creatures: Resolutions, Preparation: The Greater Glory of God)	.	37
Third	Day (The Three Sins: The Tale of Sins: Prayer: Hell)	.	71
Fourth	Day (Death and Judgment: Christ the King: Catholic Action: The Incarnation)	. .	105
Fifth	Day (The Nativity: The Two Standards: The Triple Cord: The Holy Family) . .	.	143
Sixth	Day (The Public Ministry: The Holy Eucharist: Poverty: The Sacred Heart) . . .	.	179
Seventh	Day (The Jews: Pilate: Chastity: Resolutions, Generosity)	.	215
Eighth	Day (The Cross: The Resurrection: Obedience: The Kingdom of God: Conclusion)	. .	249

CONTENTS

First. The Creator's Day: The Logos' existence

Second Day (Heavenly Charity): Resolutions. Preparation. The Greater Glory of God.

Third Day. The Three Gifts. The Tale of Sister Mary
Basil.

Fourth Day. Death and Judgement. Christ the King.
Catholic Hope. The Sacraments.

Fifth Day. The Nativity. The Two Standards. The
Triple Cord. The Holy Family.

Sixth Day. The Fourth Mystery. The Holy Mockery.
Poverty. The Sacred Heart.

Seventh Day. The Jews' Divine Liberality. Liberality
exercised.

Eighth Day. Hell. Fire. The Resurrection. Obedience.
The Kingdom of God. Conclusion.

FISRT DAY.

PREPARATION.

PATRON: St. John the Baptist.

READING: Mark IV, 1-34; Apoc. 1; Imitation
I, 20-21.

FIRST MEDITATION: Peace (External Peace, Internal Peace, Lasting Peace).

SECOND MEDITATION: God (God's Power, God's
Wisdom, God's Righteousness).

CONSIDERATION: The Light (Spiritual Notes,
Spiritual Guidance, Spiritual Warfare).

THIRD MEDITATION: Confession (Examination
of Conscience, Confession, Holy Communion).

✝

THE VOICE OF CHRIST.

'Let not Moses therefore speak to me, but Thou, Lord my God, eternal truth; lest haply I die, and be made without fruit.' — (*Imitation of Christ*, bk. III, chap. 2; cf. *The Confessions of St. Augustine*, bk. IX, chap. 25.)

Nor Moses, Lord,
   Nor any of the prophets, lest I die,
      And hearkening not to Thee, bring forth no fruit;
      They mark the route,
Thy word is strength to walk thereby.

Low is thy voice,
   Scarce heard, amid the streets' unthinking din,
      Scarce, 'mid the empty laughter and the shout:
      Tumult without,
And deadlier tumult far within.

Sweet is thy voice
   For him that heareth Thee; the charmer Thou,
      That charmeth wisely; the soul, upon thy call,
      Forgetteth all,
And following Thee, hath good enow.

O Master, Master,
   Could we be deaf to every worldlier love,
      From ever lesser thing avert our ear,
      Were that to hear
Thy welcome unto joy above?

FIRST DAY, FIRST MEDITATION:

PEACE.

WE may imagine Our Lord coming into our midst with the words: 'Peace be to you' (John XX, 19, 26). He is to be among us in a special way during our retreat. 'Peace be to this house'; it is the greeting of the priest to the household that has summoned him. We ask for that peace which the world cannot give.

EXTERNAL PEACE. Our annual retreat is a beginning, rather than an end. It belongs to the year that follows, rather than to the year that precedes. It should not be made when the religious are exhausted in mind and body, at the conclusion of their year's work, but rather when they have had something in the way of holiday, and are ready for fresh efforts. Nor is the retreat so tiring as to absorb all this fresh energy; nevertheless it should itself be followed by a period of moderate relaxation, before the main work of the year begins. Yet, if it is to be a time of effort, it is not to be a time of strain. Predominantly it should be a time of peace, a time when peace is possessed and still more peace is sought.

A retreat is peace for body and mind. As regards our body, we are removed from our ordinary occupations by obedience, but much

1 *

still depends upon ourselves. We must take care really to give them up, and all else that is likely to distract us. At other times a certain amount of intercourse, under the proper conditions, is not merely harmless, but enables all to know and love one another; but now rigid silence must be the rule. During the retreat recollection in general, but above all silence, may well be the particular subject of our examination of conscience. Not that charity must cease; rather it must increase. But for the present charity according to wisdom will confine itself to prayer, and that right earnest; prayer that each and all may draw rich fruit from the retreat. We do not know God's designs upon others, to heal and hallow; we only know for certain that we are doing the devil's work if we distract them. We should pray for them, gathered together in Christ's name with ourselves; but to do anything that hinders their peace with God is true scandal. Mutual edification can only be through silence and recollection.

A retreat would not be of much use if it bore no relation at all to our ordinary occupations. It is not merely a time in which our occupation is different. But even the thought of our ordinary occupations may easily prove very distracting. It is distracting if it hinders us from contemplating the great truths in themselves. Not that we should engage in mere abstract speculation without any ulterior purpose; but we cannot hope to apply those truths as we should, unless we have first a firm grasp upon them as they are in their own deep truth. Even where we come to their application, it must only be with a view to this that we should dwell on the daily business of our life. We must beware of unprofitable rehearsals of the past, or idle dreams of a future, unlike that which we at bottom purpose in the retreat.

INTERNAL PEACE. Peace as we have described it so far is in the main something negative; it is that not-doing and not-thinking which always requires a higher positive activity to justify it. And this activity is once again the establishment of peace, but of a peace which is not mere riddance, but rather contains within itself supreme perfection. It is divine peace, peace with God. Enmity to God means sin and punishment, hell itself if carried far enough. Sin is the one great evil, to be avoided at all costs. Yet against sin, against our own imperfections and all our weakness, we can do nothing without God's grace, of which we need a full and overflowing measure. For this we need to put ourselves into accord with Him. With this great Ally we shall come ever nearer to realising, even in this life, the real and solid peace born of complete victory.

Nothing else can satisfy us, neither riches nor pleasure, all the less so because we are religious

and have abandoned these things. Any large
indulgence in them for their own sake we have
ourselves put out of our reach, and we can only
make ourselves restless and unhappy, not to say
ridiculous, by trying to save some fragment from
that magnificent holocaust. It is to introduce
strife and discrepancy in our lives, where one
simple law should govern all. God has all to
give us, and delights to give it us. He only
asks us to draw near in loving trust. He will
give us His own peace, which no creature can
give, but only He.

Peace with God is therefore peace with ourselves. The joys and sorrows of life may come
and go, but there will be true peace beneath,
nay, even a profounder joy, that no man will
take from us. There will be no ugly compro-
mises, no imagined clash of interests. We shall
not be frightened or flustered into attempting to
disguise from ourselves our own rule of life, that
rule which is in very truth God Himself. We
shall stop to think, as so few do nowadays; and,
as still fewer do, we shall look ourselves fairly
and squarely in the face, and without sparing
ourselves, and without mere scruples, judge of
our lives according to that living Rule. And
from this will spring the strong desire to set
everything right, and to keep it so. The ways
and means must be clear, and the will firm.
Emotion is only safe when based on a proper

understanding of the matter, and a resolute will — both supported by God's grace.

We need this time, we need this peace, to right the past. We may be gradually slackening in our fervour, giving up good practices, acquiring habits which are at least grave imperfections. Our faults may be becoming more frequent. We may be in greater danger than we think. Now is the time to examine ourselves carefully, to make good the past, to be sorry and purpose amendment. All this is to draw near to God and to make or strengthen our peace with Him.

We need to provide for the future. In any case a retreat is the great time for advance. It always marks a great epoch in the spiritual life, if not of advance, then of going back, of hardening against God. If we are to be saints, it is chiefly our retreats which will make us such, they will be the flood-marks of God's graces. For this greater light and fervour we must draw near to God.

LASTING PEACE. It is now clear how important it is that we should aim at this peace, peace from all that might distract our minds, peace with and in and for God. At all times both must to some extent be the ideal of the Christian soul, for it must always endeavour to love creatures only for God's sake, and to find Him in them. In time of retreat all the time possible must be consecrated to direct intercourse

with God, and when that can be had, and in so
far as it can be had, nothing else can be thought
worth attending to. This principle must of course
be carried through with prudence, so that it be
not used as a pretext for departing from common
life, or endangering the health. For a certain
amount of time every day bodily exercise is necessary, and our minds must be relieved by distraction, by lighter but harmless thoughts, whose
end is not dissipation, but only rest and refreshment for the better conduct of the great matter
in hand. Nevertheless, if we have drunk a deep
draught of this peace, we shall not easily lose
our taste for it, even out of retreat. Internal
peace we can never afford to lose; we must ever
be ready to present ourselves in spirit or in body
before Our Blessed Lord, to do full justice, so
far as human frailty allows, to all His claims
upon us, to face Him and to face ourselves.
Nay, even temptation, even sin and guilt itself, must not scare us or estrange us from our
heavenly Father. Our repentance must be swift,
and it must be the repentance of Peter, who
never doubted of his Master's love for him, not
the repentance of Judas, who would not believe
that there was forgiveness for him. External
peace we cannot secure in the same measure
outside retreat as in it; and again, the work
allotted to some individuals is of a more distracting kind than that allotted to others. But all

need to relish internal peace, to be interior men, men of prayer and recollection; their outward activity will not be hallowed unless, like Moses, they come to the multitude from the presence of God. If this spirit be preserved, outward practice will not go very far wrong. Spiritual duties will be faithfully performed; if they too come to be rushed, then we are indeed burning the candle at both ends. Silence will to some extent be preserved, according to the work prescribed; a mere chatterbox will never have much to show for himself, even should he be given work that really calls for a good deal of conversation; and much less, of course, if it does not. Let us cultivate the calm yet strenuous patience which comes of internal peace, eschewing fussiness and rush no less than idle flippancy; let us always be recollected, true lovers of silence, because true lovers of God and mindful of His presence, glad to be able to practise it when duty imposes it, and learning then all that should most appear in our conversation.

FIRST DAY, SECOND MEDITATION:

GOD.

We may endeavour to picture to ourselves such a scene as Isaiah saw, the Lord sitting upon a throne, with winged seraphim that cry, Holy, Holy, Holy (Isai. VI); or that vision of the

Seer of Patmos, wherein the four living beasts
take up the same homage (Apoc. IV). We pray
that our puny minds may have an increased
understanding of the infinite God, from whom
our retreat makes its beginning. There is one
Being with whom we must reckon, and only
one; that is a good thought with which to begin
a retreat.

Almighty God is a pure and simple Essence,
a single and immeasurable Act of Being. But
our very finite understanding cannot directly conceive such a Being; we have to resort to many
shifts, to approach Him from many sides, if we
are even to begin to realise Him. And now we
make our first effort. We start from God's great
attributes of power, wisdom, holiness; we do not
endeavour formally to prove His existence by
way of these, yet we review the arguments
themselves in order to strengthen and clarify
our conception of Him. To God's power, wisdom, holiness we may attach our own faith,
hope, charity; we may even take the Persons of
the Blessed Trinity in corresponding order. To
His power, again, is more especially due our
praise and reverence, to His wisdom our service,
while we may consider our end, our own salvation, in connection with His holiness.

GOD'S POWER. There must be something self-
existing. The totality of being cannot be an
effect; various effects we see everywhere, but

somewhere there must be a cause which is no effect. It is ridiculous to suppose that we can do away with dependence by multiplying the things dependent. Sooner or later we must come to the First Cause, who is self-existing and the cause of all other existence. Nor is He the cause merely of existence, but of all the perfections that are found in existing things. The manifold beauties of nature, the wonderful harmony of its complex laws and phenomena, all that we find to love and admire in the skill and goodness of man — all these are but a faint reflection of Him who made them, of His infinite perfection and inexhaustible Being. And the creative act itself argues a power to which we can set no limit; the creature can mould or change the matter that he finds before him, but he cannot produce it out of nothing.

Like all else in this wide world, and in the whole universe, we came to exist because He spake the word. The matter of our bodies was created long ago, and our souls sprang into being when His providence had prepared their dwelling. His we are, and He alone can and does keep us from that nothingness out of which He has drawn us. The excellences of our human being proclaim the more His perfections, but without lessening our dependence. It is not merely rule or dominion that He has over us, but an ownership absolute without compare.

Either, then, we elect to have Him for our enemy, an enemy whom it is useless and wicked folly to oppose, from whose power and punish‑ment we can in no way escape; or else we may offer Him a willing and joyful service. His in‑finite power is but one aspect of His infinite perfection; infinitely perfect as He is, and the source of all perfection, He can harbour no unworthy aims, He can do no evil to those who truly try to serve Him. Nor can they on their side find anything more worthy to do. He de‑serves our confidence, our utter faith, the faith of Abraham and Paul. Indeed, in this life He grants us that peace and joy of which we have been speaking, a first instalment of the full pos‑session of Himself in the next. If servants are proud of their lord, or children of their father, far better cause have we to exult in the Lord our God, and in the merciful love He bears His creatures. Thus we realise His power, but in such a way as to reverence and praise Him.

GOD'S WISDOM. But He has set us in the world, and the world gives us fresh thoughts about Him. We find it rich in variety, yet wonderfully uniform in types. We find great departments of being, separated off each from the other by impassable barriers, each of which came into being in a manner wholly unaccounted for by existing laws of nature, marvellous as these latter are themselves in their vast sweep and mutual adjustment. Even in the vegetable kingdom, nay, even in things without life, we find a bewildering complexity of structure; what then shall we say of man, whose body alone is the subject, not of one, but of a hundred sciences, while his mind baffles them all? When we come into a room and find everything ready for our purpose, whether it be food or work or rest we desire, we naturally ask who has thus carefully and skilfully divined our least wish, and we should ridicule the idea that the party responsible was just nobody and nothing. And when we consider the nice adjustment of the human body, of air and temperature and other natural conditions, of animal and vegetable species, and of the heavenly bodies, we are speechless at the vast forethought exerted for our sakes, and the profusion of the supreme Deviser.

But our thoughts must travel farther, into past and future. That same Wisdom guides our path from beginning to end, and all other men's, and all our mutual intercourse. Of His free will He has chosen each of us, and prepared our way, out of a multitude of possible men and possible careers. Some graces, such as creation and redemption, we hold in common with all mankind, some in common with fewer, some are all our own. But for us individually they make up one great whole, God's guidance of our life, foiled in part by our own fault, but ever re-asserting itself, and still with us in this supreme business of a retreat. And if He has been lavish to us upon our journey, much greater will be the lavishness of His divine welcome at the journey's end, and of those everlasting joys which eye hath not seen nor ear heard.

And so we feel enkindled our hope and courage, for not merely has our heavenly Maker good designs upon us, but they are carefully worked out to the last detail by One whom nothing can escape, who gives us ample light and ample strength, if we will but use it. And He through whom all things were made, Everlasting Wisdom, is always dwelling in the Church, His Mystical Body, ready to administer His graces with more especial efficacy through her, and indeed to administer even Himself, as He is also eager to welcome us one day into the company of the Blessed to enjoy Himself more perfectly. It is His Wisdom that brings us to Himself, and the thought of it fills us with joyful desire to serve Him.

GOD'S RIGHTEOUSNESS. For this life of ours has a purpose, and a good purpose. We are bound to reflect upon the meaning of existence; but we can find no meaning in it, unless we know God's purpose in bestowing it upon us. And from His infinite perfection and goodness, as has been said, we can know that it comes to us as a blessing. Nor can we doubt that the righteous God desires that we should be righteous. Clearly our blessing must lie in virtue. But that blessing has a here and a hereafter; hereafter, when once attained, it cannot be lost, but here we can cast it away if we will, and if we cast it away, we cast away our hereafter with it.

Our life, then, is a probation, but a probation wherein God in His goodness gives us every help to righteousness; and not merely to that natural virtue which alone our nature demands, but to supernatural holiness, to that state of supernatural grace to which we have no possible right, the adoption of sons imparted to us through the Saviour's death and resurrection, the membership of His Mystical Body, confirmed by the life-giving reception of His Body and Blood — all this and much more, leading to the vision of His infinite glory. In the face of such spurs and helps it is a little thing to say that God is faithful to His promises, and will not allow us to be tempted above our strength. Rather let us remember that the trials of this life are not worthy to be compared to the glory which shall be revealed in us, if we suffer with Christ, that with Him we may be glorified.

But God is not mocked. He desires our welfare and salvation, and makes our path sweet and easy unto it; but woe betide those who scorn these vast mercies! His righteousness turns

His power and His wisdom against those who
defy Him to the end, and their worm dieth not.
On this we shall think yet again later; suffice
it here that it helps us to understand God a
little better, and to take our task more seriously.

God, then, hates evil, as He loves good. And
we must follow Him in this, but always, like
Him, wishing all men here below to be saved,
detesting the sin, whether in self or neighbour,
but none the less loving our neighbour as our-
self. We must endeavour to root out all evil
in ourselves, that we may be better conformed
to God's holiness; in proportion as we do this,
we shall also be working good in others, directly
if God call us to a directly apostolic life, but
in any case by prayer and example. We are
called to be the outward expression, the very
embodiment of God's goodness to man, that
through us and in us they may come to know
and love Him who has loved them first. And
the consummation of holiness is salvation; the
end set before us is that we should finally be
sanctified by the vision of Holiness Itself.

FIRST DAY, CONSIDERATION:

THE LIGHT.

'Everyone that doth evil hateth the light, and
cometh not to the light, that his works be not
convicted. But he who doth the truth cometh

to the light, that it be made plain that his works have been wrought in God' (John III, 20-21).

SPIRITUAL NOTES. 'Know thyself!' From of old it has been accounted a point of wisdom. To look oneself squarely in the face, to gauge one's own character, one's evil propensities, and the efforts which one is making to combat them, all this is difficult and disagreeable; nevertheless, strictly speaking, there was no need of revelation or religious rules to tell us that it is a wise thing to do. How few, for example, make sure that they realise their own motives! Even in religion it is possible to act first, and find a plausible motive afterwards; perhaps the real motive is a little too ugly to look at. How quickly personal considerations make themselves felt, especially with more sensitive natures! It is not an easy matter to make the desire for God's glory exercise effective control. But the first step is to take stock of the facts, to form an accurate estimate of the forces at work and their relative power. And the result is sure to be of permanent value to us, and is therefore worth noting down, lest we straightway forget what manner of men we are. Other notes there may be of a spiritual kind, either for our own or others' benefit; but it is good to keep a strictly personal record. There is a danger of drifting, of passing from day to day — and how quickly the days flit by — without ever stopping

to ask ourselves seriously how we stand. And
so at the end of a long period, say in our annual retreat, when we come to take stock of
ourselves, we may find that we have been in a
more or less comatose condition, whence we have
some trouble to rouse ourselves. This means
sheer waste of time, of time that is all too pre-
cious, waste of time and waste of light and grace
which the Divine Mercy has given us. We must
train ourselves to live on the *qui vive,* and one
of the surest means of doing this is to take
careful note of what passes within the soul. It
is hard to kick against the goad. The clear
statement of a problem often brings the answer;
the clear statement of our thoughts and feelings
will often force us, as it were, to act. Are there
not moments when it seems but a little thing
to become a saint, when it seems that we had
been so long ere this, had we but made up our
minds to go straight ahead once the way was
clear, to offer to God promptly and generously
whatever He should clearly desire of us? And
to take careful note of His inspirations is one
chief effect of a resolve to lose nothing of the
divine gift.

We may feel keenly some objections to notes
of this kind. Perhaps we have read some left
by others, and have thought them unreal, or at
least too airy and sentimental to be the result
of any strong movement of intellect or will. Or

we may have a very proper dread of writing for posterity. The remedy for all this is to take pains to follow a right method. Notes of this kind should be short, terse, unaffected. We should not write until we are quite sure what it is that we have to write, and then we should write it briefly and accurately, with the date. In this way we can be sure that it will have a permanent value for us. We shall be turning our experience to the best possible account for present and future profit. We shall be in the best possible position to know what the Divine Goodness would have us do, and to accomplish it with all our strength.

SPIRITUAL GUIDANCE. The advantages derived from spiritual notes are derived tenfold from spiritual direction. Two heads are better than one; much as we can profit from a calm and accurate survey of our own state, we can profit far more by associating with ourselves in that survey an able helper. Evidently, too, the danger of drifting is reduced to a minimum when at regular intervals we try to give to another the clearest account of ourselves that we can. And it becomes far more difficult not to answer to grace once we have laid open to another what it is that we feel is asked of us. Spiritual direction, however, takes us much farther than spiritual notes, and confers benefits of its own. Sometimes we may need a friendly warning that we are clutching at a phantom, that we are seeking to turn aside from the only true road, the road of renunciation and mortification, the royal road of the holy Cross. Or we may not understand the Divine Will in respect of the regular ordering of our lives. Our perfection lies in the exact observance of our rule, and it can only be an evil delusion to imagine that it is an indifferent matter to depart from it in any way, except of course with the sanction of the proper authority. These and other wrong notions may enter our heads, and unless they make a speedy exit there will be much waste of time and effort. Again, from time to time the soul is the better for positive encouragement. The *labor certaminis* of which the Imitation speaks — quoting from Quintilian — the weariness of the struggle, may at times dishearten us, and a kind word may be a consolation and a blessing.

There is also the merit of obedience. Spiritual direction in some form or another has always been the rule among those who have followed the counsels. It was recognised to be a difficult task to steer one's path aright between the two extremes of indiscretion and laxity. And so there is always a more or less official direction to be had. The recent code of Canon Law (Canon 530), while strictly forbidding all religious superiors to do anything to induce their subjects to manifest their conscience to them, on the other hand encourages subjects to explain their doubts and difficulties to their superiors, if these latter be priests. But this legislation with regard to superiors does not touch the general question of the need of spiritual guidance. We shall merit by submitting to direction in a humble and obedient spirit; we shall certainly suffer for it if we are resolved to gang our own gait. We shall be withdrawing ourselves from God's admirable light, and perhaps letting ourselves in for all manner of faults and follies.

To complain that spiritual direction leads to want of self-reliance, and so forth, is to misunderstand the whole purpose both of spiritual direction and of the spiritual life as a whole. The religious must learn, not to abdicate his judgment, but to form it on sound lines. Neither can he abdicate his will. No one can fight his battles for him; he must ever learn to strive more manfully, to win great battles when all is against him, and for the purest motives, certainly not therefore in any dependence upon encouragement or praise of man. His director must not get between him and his God. No doubt, as time goes on, there is as a matter of fact less need for constant reference to others; yet even in human affairs the experienced and the truly wise are not above consulting their fellows, even though humility be no large part of their wisdom.

Besides spiritual direction in the strict sense, much profitable spiritual guidance may be found in spiritual exhortations and instructions of various kinds, and in spiritual reading. Evidently exhortations and instructions should be made much of; to avoid them is often to shun the light. Spiritual reading should be carefully chosen from the ample field available. Holy Scripture is the spiritual reading provided for us by Almighty God: no one can go very wrong in his ideas who knows and loves the Imitation of Christ: Father Rodriguez has a great and deserved vogue, though in a certain number of places he has the Society exclusively, or almost exclusively, in view: the lives of the Saints also have their lessons, but the number of well-written lives is small.

SPIRITUAL WARFARE. Evidently the subject matter of spiritual notes and of spiritual guidance is our whole spiritual warfare. It is what we are, what we are doing, or not doing, what we are experiencing. As we proceed, we come to see more clearly what are the things that chiefly matter, at all events, for us. But from the first we may safely adopt a few general principles as to the relative importance of different items. And first of all comes what is most fundamental in our religious life, our vocation itself. The first thing is to remain steadfast in our God-given purpose to follow the life of the counsels in our order. Of course, a time may come when it is better both for the order and for the religious that he should quit it; the interests of the two coincide in this matter, and it is as much to the interest of superiors as of subjects not to delay a desirable departure. But the possibility of sheer temptation must also be recognised; if in all other matters, why not in this? If the devil can induce one who ought to be living in religion to abandon it, he has brought his whole spiritual life on to a lower sphere, and has gained many victories in one. For the fervent religious, then, who is aiming seriously at perfection, and normally finds his peace and joy in the special state to which he has been called, temptations of this sort will be no more a cause of surprise or alarm than those of other kinds. We cannot prescribe, we cannot always foresee, our own temptations; we must take them as they come, and trust in the Lord.

After our vocation, the vows contain what is most fundamental. They will be treated individually in later considerations, and it is enough to say here that if they are safe, everything is safe. It is their observance which makes a religious; their better observance makes the better religious. Other points there are, which also have to be looked to carefully. Spiritual duties must be faithfully and fervently discharged; they

are the chief means of grace. Time-saving devices have no place here, and can only work
mischief; any such temptation must be resisted
stoutly, best of all by somewhat lengthening the
time, where feasible. Penances, too, may run to
indiscretion if not properly authorised. Finally,
anything that is on our mind should be brought
to the light, that whatever good there be in it
may be matured, and evil repressed.

But evidently our spiritual enlightenment and
education exists, not merely in dealing with isolated phenomena, but in learning to recognise
the workings of God's Spirit within ourselves
quickly and easily. And we must beware of the
devil's wiles, seeing that he can transform himself into an angel bearing the appearance of that
same heavenly light. Thus, the lax and coarse
conscience, which makes little of defects and
what it calls peccadilloes, he endeavours to make
coarser still. But against the more sensitive soul,
that shrinks from sin with horror, a more subtle
artifice is needed, namely, to make it believe
that it has already sinned where really it has
not. This conflict of his suggestion with inward
conviction that one has not sinned constitutes
a scruple in the strict sense, and unless the soul
submit to guidance it may produce trouble. We
should try to ensure in ourselves a true and
accurate estimate of sin, whether we tend to the
one extreme or the other. Highly strung, sensi-

tive and more or less neurotic natures are naturally prone to scruples; with them, speaking broadly, introspection should be reduced to a minimum, and largely replaced by a wise direction, at once firm and gentle. To say that all is imagination, for instance, may be a correct diagnosis of the disease, but certainly not a cure. On the other hand introspection cannot wholly be done away with, whatever the subject or temperament. Some kind of examination of conscience will always remain indispensable, and some lessons gathered from it, for example, that certain trains of thought are apt to end in sheer temptation. A little care can prevent what introspection is really needful from being converted into morbid broodings, or otherwise taking a perilous turn.

Depression may also come, or, as it is more affectionately called, 'the dumps'. This may be due to many causes, natural or supernatural. We should try to discover which of them is at work, and behave accordingly. In any case it is an experience to be lived bravely through, but not a time for epoch-making resolutions. For those clearer weather is needed.

FIRST DAY, THIRD MEDITATION:

CONFESSION.

Under this heading we propose to speak both of amendment and of the sacrament, for the two are closely connected, and are both the fruit of contrition, with which we are at present largely concerned. With confession it is natural to take the examination of conscience, which indeed in some shape or other is essential to it; with this we shall begin. And afterwards we shall go on to speak of the practice of Holy Communion under certain aspects which are connected with confession, reserving a more profound treatment of the Holy Eucharist for a later time.

EXAMINATION OF CONSCIENCE. This comprises the particular and the general examination; we may speak first of the former, which, if anything, is the more important of the two. The practice is simple enough, and need not delay us. It is intended for the extirpation of some particular defect. We advert to this defect when we rise, proposing with God's grace to guard against it; and in our midday and night examinations of conscience we notice and record how many times we have fallen, and whether we are improving. Evidently it will help if we make a fall something of an event, performing some slight penance in atonement, and even making some gesture to imply repentance at once, if it can be done without attracting attention.

Such is the particular examen, and it must be evident that, properly used, it can become a tremendous force in our lives. Even if our characters were nothing, so to speak, but a fortuitous concurrence of atoms, a mere bundle of qualities without any underlying unity, *divide et impera* — divide to master — would still be the best rule. It would still be wisdom to tackle our defects one by one, and while striving conscientiously for all-round perfection, to concentrate our more especial attention upon one definite item. But in point of fact it is far otherwise. There is a great unity in a man's character. The good traits and the bad traits have a close relation among themselves and to each other. He will certainly have the defects of his virtues. So true is this, that for most there is practically but one serious danger. The road to ruin for any single soul is usually a very definite one, and fairly easy to predict. There is a root-vice, that not only dwarfs but goes far towards explaining the rest. The need of concentration is thus ten times greater. It is at this 'ruling passion' that we need to strike, to strike hard and to strike home. There is but one security for us, in so far as there is any; it is to make our weak point our strongest and safest. In what touches it we must be almost unreasonably severe in refusing to avail ourselves of any excuse or evasion. There is no other way, if we are in earnest; the rule is simple and drastic, and contains the most profound wisdom. But it needs all the resources of the particular examen to carry it into effect.

It thus becomes of some consequence, even for the particular examen, to be sure of one's ruling passion. This is a subject to which we shall have to return later, and it is enough to say here that from the meditation on our tale of sins, and from our past examinations of conscience, especially those for confession, we may even now have a fairly clear idea of it. Perhaps we have been reasonably certain about it for some time. The question then arises, what form is the particular examen to take? Not that it is an absolutely inviolable rule that the two should be connected; charity, good discipline or the like may occasionally require that an external fault should be corrected at once, even though it have no great significance in our spiritual life. In any case we should pitch upon something external and tangible, if possible one of the worst habits in which the root-vice expresses itself. Only difficulties against chastity cannot be treated in this way; it is better to grapple with them indirectly, making our examination on our watch over the senses, mortification or the like. Mortification would be an example of the use of the examination for a positive purpose, instead of the more usual repression of faults. It may at times put more life into the exercise to perform an act of a particular virtue so many times a day, or something of that kind.

The general examination of conscience is a great aid to self-knowledge, which the particular examen in the main presupposes. Its more immediate end, however, is the cleansing of the conscience. We thank our Heavenly Father for His graces and blessings since our last examen, taking in also one or two greater favours of the past, general or particular. We ask for knowledge of our sins, for contrition and a firm purpose of amendment. First we attend to the particular, and then to the general examination. We may find it a help, especially for confession, to keep a record even of the latter. We make several fervent acts of contrition, including perfect contrition; that is the vital point. Vocal prayers may be inserted, and other points observed which will be touched upon later in the consideration on prayer. The frequent recurrence of offences of a particular kind, even though mere imperfections, might be a sign that we should take them for our particular examen. Some attempt should be made to foresee dangerous occasions.

CONFESSION. Confession is a subject about which religious should be peculiarly well-informed, not merely for their own sake but their neighbour's. Children need to be most carefully instructed on the point, and grown-up Catholics are often the better for an accurate explanation both of doctrine and practice. This, however, is not the place for a full treatment of the subject, and only one or two points will be touched upon. Here we should bestow even greater care upon acts of contrition, acts of perfect contrition and even unreserved perfect contrition, covering even the slightest offence that can truly be called sin, even though we do not happen to think of it. This is the policy of the clean slate; for as long as we retain an attachment to any particular kind of venial sin, the venial sins thus unrepented of cannot be forgiven, either by perfect contrition or confession. The perfect contrition wipes out all sins for which we are sorry, and confession has the like power even if there be but attrition, that is, sorrow arising from fear of punishment or hope of reward; but the sins must be renounced, otherwise their malice endures. In the case of mortal sin, of course, it would be different; there can be no perfect contrition that leaves a mortal sin unrepented, no valid confession that leaves it unconfessed.

During the annual retreat it is a good thing to make a general confession, unless it be the custom to choose some other time. Generally speaking, it will be best to confess the sins of the past year, with two or three chief sins of one's past life. But there is no obligation thereto, and it may at times happen that a religious is easily though needlessly disturbed in mind by such a review of the past, in which case it is

best to omit it, and to persevere in the calm
and happy service of God, perhaps with a resolution to make one's peace of mind more secure. If on the other hand he thinks that there
is serious ground for anxiety in what has happened
even farther back, the best thing he can do is
to explain the whole matter in confession, and
abide by the confessor's decision. There can
only be an actual obligation to go back upon
previous confessions if one is reasonably sure
that one has failed to confess what one was
reasonably sure was a mortal sin.

Before leaving the subject of confession, it
may be worth while to give a brief summary
of the canons of the new Code that deal with
the confessions of nuns. There is to be a single
ordinary confessor for every convent, to hear
the confessions ot the whole community, unless
their number or some other good reason demand more (can. 520 § 1). If any nun, for her
greater peace and progress, demand a special
confessor or director, the bishop is to grant this
without difficulty, while watching against any
abuse in the matter (can. 520 § 2). Every convent is to have an extraordinary confessor, who
shall visit the house at least four times a year,
when all the nuns must appear before him, if
only to receive his blessing (can. 521 § 1). The
bishop is to appoint some priests for each convent, to whom the nuns may go to confess

without difficulty in particular cases, without
having to ask the bishop's leave (can. 521 § 2).
If any nun asks for any of these confessors, the
superioress is not to make the slightest attempt
to find out the reason, or make the slightest
difficulty (can. 521 § 3). Notwithstanding all
that precedes, if any nun for the peace of her
conscience confess to a confessor approved for
women by the bishop in any church or oratory,
even a semi-public oratory, that confession is
valid and lawful, and the superioress may not
prevent or in any way enquire about such a confession, nor is the nun bound to report anything
of the matter to the superioress (can. 522). With
regard to this canon, it may be remarked, (1) that
although the nun's confession, to be lawful, should
be in some sense for the peace of her conscience,
the non-fulfilment of this condition would not in-
validate the confession; (2) the convent chapel
itself is a semi-public oratory within the meaning
of the canon; (3) all confessors in England usually
have faculties for women, but this is not always
the case elsewhere; it is not the case in Rome
itself, where faculties for men alone are sometimes given at first. Finally, a nun who is
seriously ill, even though not in danger of death,
may send for any confessor approved for women,
and confess to him as often as she will, while
the sickness lasts; nor is the superioress in any
way whatever to stop her doing so (can. 523).

HOLY COMMUNION. It is natural to add a few words on Holy Communion. It is chiefly important that the papal decree on daily communion should be read as prescribed, and be carefully listened to and understood. One point is worth insisting on. Perhaps the chief argument employed against daily communion before the decree was the danger of too great familiarity and want of reverence. This may serve as a warning. Under all circumstances at least a quarter of an hour should be spent in devout preparation, and again afterwards in thanksgiving, both if possible there where we communicate. It will, of course, be a help to vary somewhat from time to time the mode of preparation and thanksgiving. Acts of Faith, Hope and Charity should always precede and follow; and some help will be found in the second meditation of the sixth day, which is devoted to the Holy Eucharist. As in the case of confession, apostolic motives should move all to secure accurate knowledge of all that concerns Holy Communion. This is especially true of those who have to deal with children. Children should frequent the holy table as soon as they have sufficient knowledge and understanding for this, but careful instruction on the subject should, of course, continue to be given them for long afterwards. It is monstrous to suppose that what is enough for a child of seven is enough for a Catholic to

go through life with. Here, as in the case of
confession, it is most important that children be
thoroughly instructed in the drill, if we may
so call it, of receiving the Sacrament. In the
case of Holy Communion this mainly consists of
learning to keep the head thrown a little back,
the eyes shut, the mouth open fairly wide, the
tongue extended a little over the lower teeth
and resting quietly. When the Blessed Sacrament has been received, no sudden movement
should be made, but the tongue should be drawn
back gently and the head brought slightly forward. The Sacred Host should be swallowed
whole when sufficiently moistened. Instruction
is also needed, not merely in the doctrine of
indulgences, but in the practical gaining of them.
A plenary indulgence should be gained every
Communion; this is best ensured by the regular
recital of a translation of the *En Ego* ('O good
and sweetest Jesus') before some representation
of Jesus crucified. Habitual weekly confession
suffices for all Communions during the week;
any translation duly authorised by a diocesan
bishop may be used, and five Our Father's and
five Hail Mary's should be said afterwards for
the Holy Father's intentions. These latter always include the progress of the Faith and some
other such intentions, but it is enough to pray
simply 'for the Holy Father's intentions', without
adverting to any of them in particular. The

En Ego and the Our Father's and Hail Mary's should not merely be run through in mind, but the prayer should be framed by the lips. This may suffice as a short practical instruction for gaining a plenary indulgence every Communion. The standard work on indulgences is that by Fr. Beringer, S. J., especially approved by the Sacred Congregation of Indulgences and translated from the German into several languages.

SECOND DAY.

THE END OF MAN.

PATRON: St. Ignatius.

READING: Mark X, 17-45; Apoc. II-III; Imitation I, 22, 25.

FIRST MEDITATION: Reverence (Reverence for God, Reverence for others, Reverence for self).

SECOND MEDITATION: Creatures (Their End, Indifference, Delusions).

CONSIDERATION: Resolutions: Preparation (Principles of Election, The Light of Experience, Method).

THIRD MEDITATION: The Greater Glory of God (Perfection, The Rule of Life, Delusions).

✠

THE MESSENGER OF THE COVENANT.

(Luke III, 4 ff.; Isaiah XL, 3 ff.; Malachy III, 1 ff.)

Prepare for Him!
A Monarch holdeth way:
No beetling pride must frown disdain,
No roughness stay
Messiah's progress to unending reign.

'Make straight His path',
In Judah's waste hath cried
The herald sent before His face:
Who shall abide
The purging fire within the holy place?

Let all flesh see
And turn from manifold sin:
Ere Jordan the cheered throng release,
Lord, enter in,
And cleanse for Thee the city of Thy peace!

———

SECOND DAY, FIRST MEDITATION:

REVERENCE.

THIS meditation is a further development of the meditation upon Almighty God, that is to say, of the first point, for the thought of God's power leads us to reverence and praise. And there is especial need to dwell upon the thought of reverence. Irreverence is one of the characteristics of our age. Socialism and other forces are tending to instil into high and low an active resentment towards any that presume to command them, a veritable instinct of contempt for all authority; while those who hold any responsible position think it well, or at all events find it necessary, to bring themselves down to the level of those they employ or govern. There is an increasing demand that leaders should be hail-fellow-well-met with the led, and should, if possible, be 'Tom', 'Dick' or 'Harry' to them as well.

Evidently there is a bad element in these tendencies. They make for inefficiency and bad morale, even for class war and revolution. True charity does not destroy discipline, but is based upon it. Just as in the Church St. Paul bids every member of Christ's Mystical Body discharge his own function in harmony with the rest, so in every other organisation those in authority must

have their position recognised and must enjoy
a proper freedom of action.

Now it would be folly to suppose that these
tendencies, so laden with irreverence, may be
left out of account in religious life. The religious is the creature of his age; he has
brought its tendencies with him into religious
life, to be doctored therein according to their
merits. A large number of religious, too, are
in direct and indirect communication with life
and thought outside, and feel much of its influence. Normally we may presume that a strong
and dangerous tendency in the world outside will
also need careful watching and counter-acting in
religion.

REVERENCE FOR GOD. 'Man', says St. Ignatius, at the outset of his Spiritual Exercises, 'was
created to praise the Lord our God, to show Him
reverence, and to serve Him, and by so doing
to save his own soul.' It is characteristic of the
Saint to lay stress on praise and reverence, for
he treated the Divine Majesty with all the cour-
tesy and etiquette of a true hidalgo; and it is
indeed fundamental, the only sure foundation for
all that follows. We cannot even begin to understand the miracle of divine love and mercy
which we are later to contemplate, except in so
far as we have realised God's infinite dignity
and holiness. Nor can we ourselves feel a true
love, or at all events the right sort of love, for

God, unless we have learned to reverence Him. In that respect we are like boys with their master; weakness in this latter is usually fatal, not merely to fear, but also to that love which casts out fear.

In view of what was said in the introduction to this meditation, it appears most useful, at all events in a short retreat like the present, to confine our attention to reverence, which will certainly bring praise in its wake. The saving of our soul will naturally be a prominent thought when we come to reflect upon death and judgment and the like. There is, of course, a certain difficulty in working up a feeling of reverence on more or less abstract grounds. Those grounds which in the main have been considered in the meditation upon God and may with profit be recalled, convince us intellectually; but in practice it is now the outward act itself that will most effectively strengthen the inward sentiment within us. We may notice, too, that in this point, as in all others, it is good to put into execution at once, so far as the circumstances of the retreat allow, any resolves that effect our whole line of conduct in any particular. The most helpful form of meditation, then, will probably be to examine ourselves on this very point of reverence towards God, and chiefly as regards the outward manifestation of it. Then we can enforce the lesson by also examining

into our reverence for others, and for our own
selves; reverence, like charity, is primarily directed to God, but is also directed to creatures
because of Him, seeing them in Him and Him
in them.

Reverence to God is above all to be shown
during prayer, whether public or private. Obviously prayer should not be scamped, but should
receive the full time allotted to it or which it
reasonably requires. The desire to save time at
the expense of prayer is the cancer of the spiritual
life, and should be stamped out remorselessly. If
it is our constant aim to be a minute earlier at
the next meal, or whatever follows — well, perhaps we shall succeed; and we shall have had
our reward. Almighty God will cut down His
graces to us if we begin to cut down our service of Him. Hence St. Ignatius is careful to
prescribe that, if we find ourselves tempted to
give less than the proper time to prayer, we
should actually give more; and indeed, it is best
always to do something extra in this respect,
even though it be but a little and not even
daily. It keeps up a spirit of generosity, and
safeguards what is actually prescribed. In the
liturgy the rubrics should be accurately and
reverently observed; a service that is all jerk
and gabble and rush profits neither priest nor
people. The singing should be to the mind of
the Church. Such is the strong bond of mind

and matter, that every piece of music is charged with an emotion of its own, and it is desecration to set sacred words to tunes that are the natural expression of flippancy or lasciviousness. In private prayers reverence should still be carefully observed; it is useless, for example, to settle oneself comfortably in an arm-chair and then announce to Almighty God that we are now ready for our trip to the seventh heaven.

Outside of prayer, also, a certain reverence needs to be shown to the Divine Majesty; we must not make sport of sacred things or laugh, to put it in a word, on the wrong side. A laugh is not its own justification, but one has to consider also what are the views and ideals that it tends to strengthen or weaken.

REVERENCE FOR OTHERS. True reverence for God, like true love of God, is offered to Him, not merely as He is in Himself and directly, but also in His creatures, in so far as they bear His authority or reflect His excellence. Almighty God remains the real and, in a sense, the only object of our reverence, but we reverence man in Him and Him in man. We reverence in this way both superiors, equals and inferiors.

Superiors, we may say, are to be reverenced most of all, because they alone have actually authority from God. In this matter we have to keep a tight hold upon the supernatural, because there is so much to make us relax our grip.

The superior is a human being like ourselves, with human failings. It is easy to notice his weaknesses and make a jest of them, easier still, perhaps, to comment upon them in a less friendly way; and there may be real faults to tempt us to such liberties. But all this will make the supernatural view of our superior all the more difficult, and obedience harder; and where we ourselves are to blame in the matter, we cannot expect any very abundant outpouring of grace to safeguard us. Submission to superiors based on the supposition that they are to be perfect is worthless; but a scrupulous reverence in matters external, whether to present or absent superiors, will bring the supernatural aspect of the matter more vividly home to us. We must see in the superior the representative of Christ, bearing authority from God, whatever He may be like personally. We may remark in passing that some characters are naturally prone to idolise superiors, and sometimes equals, or even inferiors — to fasten upon some individual and resolutely believe him perfect, in fact, a veritable saint. This is a very dangerous tendency, for there is no one without his faults, and the final discovery of them may give the idoliser a terrible shaking.

Our equals must also be treated with reverence. They are not mere mates in a common job, but religious called to perfection. We ought to esteem their high vocation no less than our own, to desire that they should live true to it no less than ourselves. We should therefore show outward respect to our brethren; perpetual frivolity tends to make all forget those spiritual principles which alone give a meaning to our lives. Overmuch familiarity, needless to say, is still more dangerous, and might ultimately bring the second vow into jeopardy.

Our inferiors are committed to us by Almighty God, and are to be formed according to His holy Will. Evidently they are not to be regarded as playthings, to amuse or entertain us, or to serve our advantage in any other way. This, of course, primarily refers to children, but can be applied in measure to others under our care. Nor should we go with the crowd in making a butt of any one; that would not merely be want of charity, but desperately bad training. Personal ridicule of the kind that hurts seldom, if ever, serves a good purpose, and on the other hand, they are few who do not need some form of encouragement. Again, we need to raise those in any way under our charge to God; so often we can help them much, if we are not afraid to give expression to holy thoughts. Above all things we need to set before them, not merely their own sanctification, but an apostolic ideal; it is the best spur to moral courage, of which the young stand so sorely in need, and indeed all whose life is to a considerable extent spent in common. The best way to steel oneself against the bogey of public opinion is to resolve to do something oneself to mould that opinion.

REVERENCE FOR SELF. We owe a certain reverence to ourselves, that is, to the work of God within us, and to His designs. We have to esteem our religious vocation, and with humility must go a sense of the divine call. Perhaps we can most easily understand the need of this reverence by considering the case where it is absent. 'I'm no saint', says a religious; and a cloak of mock-humility is thrown over laxity and tepidity, and things are left undone which would be far from entailing heroic virtue. 'I'm only a duffer'; all difficult and exacting work is declined. Now we should, of course, beware of over-estimating our natural talents, and still more of over-estimating our virtues; nevertheless these things come from God, and we should be ready to use them to the utmost in His service, even while confessing that of ourselves we are nothing. The mere fact that we are acting under obedience should make us feel confident that we shall have our heavenly Father's help, even if the effort appears to overtax our powers; we need plenty of dash and hope if we are to be His worthy sons. Many motives, it is true, urge us to this, but it is obvious that reverence is one of them; we must not treat with sheer contempt all that has been given us. That is mock-humility, a cowardly substitute that makes a failure of Almighty God.

It is always bad to play the buffoon, even with equals, but still more with inferiors. It prevents good work and good influence. No doubt, humiliations are good for us, but much discretion has to be exercised in seeking them. Speaking broadly, regard for the state and the work to which God has called us forbids us positively to aim at being a laughing-stock.

SECOND DAY, SECOND MEDITATION:

CREATURES.

He hath given His angels charge over thee,
   To keep thee in all thy ways;
In their hands they shall bear thee up,
   Lest thou dash thy foot against a stone.   (Ps. 90.)

Even as Satan showed Our Lord the kingdoms of the earth and their glory, so we may imagine our Angel Guardian displaying them to us. Or again, we may picture ourselves looking down from a height upon some great city, such as our own metropolis. We behold the human beings, that seem like so many busy ants, the great buildings that dwarf them, the traffic and the commerce, and all that men's desires have put together and maintain; and almost in bewilderment we ask our heavenly guide what it

all means, what we have to do with it all, and
how we are to demean ourselves when we plunge
once more into the thick of it. And the answer
is, that this is the field, these the means devised
by the Wisdom of God for our service of Him;
for it was more especially to His Wisdom that,
when first meditating upon Him, we attached
our thoughts of service.

THEIR END. We find ourselves, then, but
a part, and a small part, of a great organism,
whose complications it is beyond our power to
master. There is an enormous variety in creation.
Man himself presents the greatest divergence in
a single species, a divergence extending to body
and soul, and to nations and individuals. And
in the animal and vegetable worlds, what a rich
profusion of types, such marvellous unity of
scheme preserved amid such wealth of execution!
The inanimate world has wonders all its own,
so great that they appear at times to dwarf man
himself; we forget the far greater complexity of
the structure of his body and the dignity of
immaterial being, at the sight of the multitude
of enormous bodies that go whirling through
space as though no power that is could control
or adjust their terrific movements:

> When I consider Thy heavens, the work of Thy fingers,
>   The moon and the stars, which Thou hast founded:
> What is man, that Thou art mindful of him,
>   Or the son of man, that Thou visitest him?   (Ps. 8.)

Wonderful, too, are the works of man's own hands; and for a moment he stands appalled, when through some want of care or knowledge the great forces which he has set going work havoc with the race, as though even yet to teach him that it is with his mind alone that he masters the power of nature.

But master he is:

Thou hast made him a little less than the angels,
    Thou hast crowned him with glory and honour,
And hast set him over the works of thy hands:
    Thou hast put all things under his feet,
All sheep and oxen,
    Yea, and the beasts of the field,
The birds of the air, and the fish of the sea,
    That pass through the paths of the sea.

(Ps. 8, continued.)

God is the supreme end of all things, which work together unto His glory; but man is the intermediate end of the brute creation, which cannot of itself attain to the knowledge and love of God, but only indirectly, as it were, through man. Man, however, has this same knowledge and love as his own immediate end, and cannot lawfully set himself or be set any intermediate end that is not contained in this. Man, therefore, cannot properly be called the end of his fellow-man, since his fellow-man must be moved, not by any regard for man in himself, but directly by the knowledge and love of God.

And herein we admire the vast sweep of the
Providence of God. Infinite Wisdom could not
leave the world a chaos of conflicting ends. For
Infinite Wisdom it was a little thing to foresee
and arrange the contact of every creature with
every other, and to make of the whole a path
whereby we may attain holiness in this life and
the reward of holiness hereafter. All things,
therefore, are ours, not excluding even our fellow-
men, whose relations with us are no less a part
of the divine scheme; all things are ours, whether
Paul, or Apollo, or Cephas, or the world, or
life, or death, or things present, or things to
come, all things are ours, and we are Christ's,
and Christ is God's (1 Cor. III, 21—23).

Almighty God, then, creates man for His own
greater glory, which is at the same time man's
supreme dignity and bliss; for it means the knowledge and love and service of his Creator and
Lord, first in probation and then in reward. And
Almighty God does not, as it were, turn man
loose in creation, but has prepared creation for
him, precisely with a view to this knowledge,
love and service. Consequently man himself may
have no other end in view in his contact with
creation than this very knowledge, love, service.
This is for him the only reasonable criterion of
conduct; any other is contrary to the Divine
Will, and to his own interest. In so far as creatures help to his end, he is to employ them;

in so far as they stand in the way, he is to leave them alone, or rid himself of them, as the case may be.

INDIFFERENCE. This rule, it will be seen, has a positive and a negative side; sometimes it will bid us use, and sometimes let alone. It must further determine the precise extent to which any creature is to be used, and also the kind of use to be made of it. One kind of use there is, which sounds rather tame at first hearing, but which is in very truth the most sublime of all. It is the mere consideration of creatures. It is from the beauty and excellence that we find in them that we come to have some inkling of that Beauty beyond compare and Supreme Perfection wherein we live and move and have our being. But, alas, we clutch at creatures for their own sake, and not because they lead us to God; the creature-pleasure of the moment blinds us to reason and religion. And how many such moments are there? We may think upon our daily routine, and upon our petty indulgences from hour to hour, and upon all such offences as there may be. For those who lead the active life much use of creatures is necessary; all the more care is therefore needed that such use be blameless.

It follows from what has been said, that man should make himself indifferent towards creatures, so far as their relation to his last end is not

4 *

evident. This indifference, taken in itself, is
something negative. It is not-choosing. Man
still waits; he does not at once embrace what
brings immediate pleasure or profit, but suspends
his choice. Until it is clear what God's service
requires, his will is like the tongue of a balance,
not inclining to either side. And why? Because
there is as yet no reasonable ground for pre-
ferring use to non-use, or non-use to use. The
essential point, be it well noticed, is the will,
though it is encouraging to know that every victory makes the next struggle in many ways more
easy. It is only when the will is attached to
some object quite independently of the divine
service that there can be a collision. And what
an indignity for the Divine Majesty, when a creature dares to weigh it in the balance against
aught created, perhaps even to find it wanting!
And this is done, not only in the committing of
mortal sin, but even in any deliberate imperfection. A trifle it may be, but there is witchery
in trifles, and to attain solid holiness we must
learn with St. John Berchmans to account trifles
of the highest moment. And if it be not such
a trifle, all the more need there is to stamp this
principle deeply upon our soul, that before we
know how a thing stands in respect of God's
service, we must not commit ourselves to it.

DELUSIONS. To penetrate ourselves the more
with this doctrine, it is a good thing to con-

sider some cases in which we easily forestall
the judgment of reason. 'Few', says A Kempis,
in a memorable sentence, 'are improved by
sickness; and in the same way those who travel
much rarely become holy.' Most would more
easily forego the sickness than the travel. And
yet to one full of life and energy, with a good
digestion and plenty of work on his hands,
it does not come so naturally to desire to be
dissolved and to be with Christ. To him a serious
illness may be a great reminder. And what is
our estimate of riches? Even the most prosperous
of Christians must confess that in this matter
Our Lord is something of an alarmist, and it
was scarcely to be expected *a priori* that those
who believe him to be the Uncreate Wisdom of
the Father should settle down with enthusiasm to
making their pile. Our Lord exhorted to alms,
as we can also do, but it was as an escape from
a great danger. Honour, too, success, reputation
come home to us far more even than riches;
and yet most good is done by those who care
not who gets the credit of it — or rather, who
are zealous that the glory should belong to
God alone.

Let us endeavour in this matter, as in all
others, to meet our own particular needs, to
take account of our own circumstances and propensities. Indeed, we must not merely attend
to our own character, but be content with that

character, in so far as it is God's gift to us, and not of our own perverting. It is intended, like His other gifts, as a means whereby we are to work out our salvation. And then we may think of the definite creatures and the definite actions that may most concern us, such, for example, as most inspire us with repugnance in the course of our duties. Indifference, in the sense explained above, as to our employments is extremely important, so that we may be prepared to accept readily whatever obedience has in store for us. Indifference, too, is needed as to rest from employment. A schoolboy notion of holidays may spoil much good work; the question is, how much can we do, not how much we can secure in the way of holidays. There is no sacredness in holidays, or in any particular proportion of holidays; we should take what we appear to need. And there is the supreme rest from labour; we must be resigned to an ineffective old age if God so please, and we cannot prepare for it better than by being kind to the aged. Neglect of the old people is an ugly feature in any house or individual. In all things we should keep before ourselves the highest ideals, but bring them into practice with a prosaic eye to detail, and institute a hunt for inordinate affections.

SECOND DAY, CONSIDERATION:

RESOLUTIONS: PREPARATION.

In the retreat of a religious, and especially in the ordinary annual retreat, resolutions occupy the place assigned by St. Ignatius in his Spiritual Exercises to the Election or Choice. His Exercises admit of a very wide application. If we ask for whom and for what they were primarily intended, the answer must be, for one who is still free to settle his own future, and who wishes to order it according to God's most holy will. For such a one St. Ignatius was prepared under certain circumstances to let the Exercises run to thirty days, and be given in full according to his written method. But it is evident that the Exercises, given in this way, mark the crisis of a human life, and the saint had no desire to restrict their use to a case of this kind. Where there is no question of determining a career, the object of a retreat is a more perfect life within that career. Religious, in particular, in their annual retreat endeavour to review their lives and conform them more closely to the model which the Divine Goodness sets before them. No doubt, there is always room for improvement in many departments; yet, as has been said, we must take one thing at a time, and concentrate upon that. We are so made, that there is always one fault or dangerous tendency that matters more than

all the rest, and even if this were not so, our
nature is such that it would still be wiser to
apply our particular endeavours to a single item.
Hence the importance of the resolution in a
retreat.

PRINCIPLES OF ELECTION. There is evidently
need of knowing oneself, one's own character,
one's own failings, one's own needs. If we fail
to hit the nail on the head, much effort may be
wasted, and meanwhile what most needed repression may be gathering strength. The problem,
then, is, in the first place, to know our own
weak point. It may be a fault of temper that
hinders our progress. It may be a want of obedience; perhaps we give way to bitter thoughts,
grumble before others, are slack and slovenly
in the actual execution of the command. Or
this very laziness may, in reality, be the central
point of our shortcomings. These are but a few
of the possibilities; one may be too prone to
something like softness in one's dealings with
others, one may be too touchy, and so forth.

There are several ways of endeavouring to
ascertain what is one's weak point and the best
way of dealing with it; they are not mutually
exclusive, but can be used to confirm or test
each other. They are given by St. Ignatius as
modes of making the great election or choice
referred to above, but can obviously be applied
with profit to the purpose in hand. In the first

place. God may in some way speak directly and clearly to the soul, and if the soul knows for certain the will of God, there can be no reason for further doubt or deliberation. Nevertheless, to guard against possible illusion in a matter of such importance, it will be well to apply the other methods also; if we have attained the truth, they can but confirm it.

The second way in which we may come to a decision is by observing the workings of our own soul, of which something has already been said in the consideration on 'Light', at the end. In the case of those who are trying earnestly to serve God and advance in religious perfection, the holy thoughts sent from God enter the soul sweetly and without difficulty; they please the soul most when it feels itself nearer to God, and in surrendering itself to them the soul is drawn still more powerfully to all that is divine. And this is due to the Holy Spirit, who reigns within her and, on the other hand, resents intrusions from evil sources, and moves the soul to ward them off. In the case of a resolution, then, the religious may consider what it is that appears to please the Spirit of God, who will not suffer it to find this spiritual peace and joy in a resolution that shirks the vital issue or has other such defects. But, once again, the resolution made in this way had best be further tested by the method that follows.

There is a third time in which our resolution
may be made, when there are no clear indications,
such as those given above, of the working of
God upon the soul. The reason may settle down
quietly to balance the pro's and con's of the
case, with a view to a reasoned and deliberate conclusion. It is of supreme importance to strengthen
oneself first of all in the spirit of the early
meditations, so as to desire only the will and
glory of God, and to be rid of disordered affection; it is then that, after prayer to be guided
aright, one may try to estimate on which side
the weight of argument leans, and offer the
conclusion finally embraced for the approval of
the Divine Majesty. Two further thoughts may
help us to choose aright; we may consider what
course we would wish to have adopted at the
hour of death, and what advice we would think
most profitable for an utter stranger, were his
case just the same as ours. We should naturally
try to do our best for him.

THE LIGHT OF EXPERIENCE. Such are the
three ways, or the three times, in which one may
make an election, or make resolutions. But there
are certain considerations which may enlighten
us as to the kind of resolution that we should
make, which yet have little or nothing corresponding to them in the case of an election.
A resolution, far more than an election, is a
considered verdict upon our own past, and

especially upon our immediate past; if that verdict
be an accurate one, the proper resolution to take
should be clear. Now we have help both from
without and from within to help us to judge of
our own past aright. The helps from without
are those which come from our intercourse with
others. In the first place there are superiors,
who doubtless have had occasion to point out
to us various points that required attention, faults
that needed to be cured. There is a truth which
we cannot take too much to heart, to wit, that
the defects which really matter, which really may
put us in danger, victory over which means victory all along the line — that these defects
usually remain the same our whole lives through.
If we are really in doubt as to what are our
own most perilous leanings, there is no time of
our life which may not throw some light on the
question, though the more immediate past deserves
a more careful scrutiny. Another point may be
mentioned in passing. It may happen that one
is more certain of one's character as a whole
than of the particular fault which most needs to
be taken in hand; or the reverse may be the
case. Whichever is more obvious, it should greatly
contribute to a knowledge of the other. Our
resolution should proceed from a certainty as
to both, that is, it should deal with a fault as
the outcome and expression of a character, and
as a means of amending and safeguarding it.

It is not only our superiors, however, from whom
we may have had occasion to learn our faults;
our equals, and indeed any persons at all with
whom we may have come into contact, may have
let us see what they thought our chief failing,
and this without any fault on their side, for truth
will out in many ways. And our own internal
and spiritual experience must prove of enormous
help; all our past examinations of conscience, our
confessions, our meditations, even this retreat —
all these will point one way, if our minds are
really open to evidence. We may think, again,
of what we like and dislike most in others.
Sometimes, too, there may be one particular
resolution which we cannot contemplate without
cold shivers — due in large measure, it may be,
to an uneasy consciousness that it is there that
the path of duty really lies. Various other lines
of enquiry may at times prove profitable. If
we know we have a strong point, or a main
attraction, or a point on which we are especially
sensitive — any of these may point us to the
weakness that most needs our care.

METHOD. But it is not only light that we
require, to see clearly what is wanted, both in
principle and in detail; but also generosity, to
make our holocaust complete. It is the one
supreme struggle of our daily life that we are
about to set ourselves, our veritable cross that
we are about to take up; we must pluck up

courage and smash the fault, giving ourselves
no quarter. St. Teresa is reported to have said
that a courageous soul makes greater progress
in a short time, than a cowardly soul in many
years. What was hitherto our weak point must
now become our strongest. One main resolution
is enough, dealing with the head and front of
our offence, though one or two minor ones will
do no harm. We must not waste our efforts,
nor make light of them: we must concentrate
upon the one thing that matters. The particular examination of conscience should be intimately connected with our resolution; but of
that enough has been said in the consideration
of the third day.

It is useful to write out the resolution, and
from time to time to come back to it and consider
it carefully in the course of the year. In accordance with what was said in the consideration
for the first day, it will probably be found a
help to show it to a superior or spiritual guide,
so that he may be the better able to keep us
up to the scratch. It might be drawn up very
briefly under five headings. In the first place
may be put the fault to be corrected, in a fairly
specific form: let us say a habit of grumbling
at the arrangements of superiors. In the second
place comes the particular examen, perhaps never
to make these arrangements the subject of conversation without necessity. Next, one or two

motives for making the resolutions that have
especially appealed to us, for instance, that such
conversations tend to make one discontented,
sluggish, disrespectful; or again, that time after
time this fault has been the outstanding blemish
in our daily life. Fourthly, some regular devotion
will be useful, to bring the matter home to
ourselves and keep the resolution active. We
may have some pious ejaculation or text, such
as, 'Jesus was silent'; and in Holy Communion
we might think how Christ humbled Himself,
becoming obedient unto death, and pray that
with the help of this sacrament, wherein the
memory of that death is renewed, we may follow
Him in humility and obedience. Under the fifth
heading may be placed one or two minor resolutions, if such there be. There need be no
hurry to put the finishing touch to our resolution,
which should be the matured product of our
whole retreat, but it should be drawn up as soon
as is reasonably possible, and finally adopted and
generously offered to God at least a day or two
before the end.

SECOND DAY, THIRD MEDITATION:

THE GREATER GLORY OF GOD.

We have now come to a meditation which is
one of the most important in the whole retreat.
What we have considered so far is clear, irre-

sistible, sublime; it is true Christian wisdom, God's own plan for the world. We have considered principles in their general application; now we must make them a part of ourselves. Our idea of perfection must become more concrete, and have reference to our own particular state. We desire even in the least detail to carry out the will of God. We desire to imitate His saints, whose grasp of these principles distinguished them from the ordinarily good. Seeing that we are trying to apply these same principles to our everyday life in religion, it is natural for us to think of the saints of our order, who, with the Queen of all the religious orders, intercede for us at the Divine Throne, that we may in all things understand and desire the greater glory of God. This is to be our true sanctification, for which, as was explained in the second meditation of the first day, we look from the holiness of God.

PERFECTION. Indifference we have seen, is something negative. It is a pause, a not-choosing. Now nothing negative is worth anything in itself. Merely not to have, not to be, not to do, only leaves us so much the poorer, except in so far as it may save us from evil. It cannot be an end in itself, nay, in itself it is a thing utterly empty, incapable of pleasing either God or man. If, therefore, a high value is set upon indifference, this must be rightly understood. It presupposes that our one desire is God's greater service, and that as soon as we perceive the bearing of the creature upon God's service, we give up our indifference, and either embrace or reject it accordingly, and that with vigour. It is not a void that we produce in ourselves, but if anything is to be ousted, it is to make room for something far better; that which is earthly and unworthy must become the divine or yield place to it.

God's greater glory, the entire accomplishment of His most holy Will, is indeed the only end that is worthy of man. Man demeans himself, his behaviour is irrational, when he seeks any other end; he ennobles himself when he seeks this. This is his supreme perfection. Nothing can be conceived more perfect than a really unreserved union of our will with God's. When we have that, we have all. Plainly it is a motive of universal application, it not only forbids what is evil, but is a guide to all that is good. Nor is it easy to apply it effectively; there should be no illusion about that. It is already plain that much mortification is needed in order to a proper indifference; and to carry this indifference through to the point of always choosing the greater good means boundless generosity and fire. The saints possessed this indifference, this generosity, to a heroic degree; yet can we say that even in them God's will ran absolutely

without let or hindrance? And we unheroic
creatures, so gladly blinded, so slack even where
God's will is plain, do we think that in an hour
or two we shall be ready for our halo? No, it
is a life-task that we set ourselves; nevertheless
if we but trust God, our progress will be rapid.

We must beware, then, of the gospel of ease;
the 'good easy man' who takes nothing very
seriously and is seldom uncomfortable has no
place in religion, which is meant for men who
are in grim earnest. Nor again can we trust to
sentiment. It is of course a mistake to say that
sentiment is not wanted; yet it is valuable, not
for its own sake, but as the outcome of conviction,
or as a preparatory stage to it. The Church
makes ample use of it; for example, she is an
incomparable milliner, and much else that her
enemies declare meretricious is in reality a syste-
matic attempt to appeal to the heart no less
than to the head. Faith remains the guide, the
guide of sentiment as of all else. Even efficiency
cannot be the final test of our lives, though in
practice it is a test with which we cannot afford
to dispense; if we have a work to do, we should
make every lawful effort to do it efficiently, but
we may fail through no fault of ours.

Duty, on the other hand, is in a different
category; it may well be our watchword at this
stage, though gradually it is to be swallowed up
in consecration and self-devotion. In these early

meditations let us make the most of the motive
of duty, our duty to God, not making of it a
favour to others, or mistaking mere politeness
for true indebtedness, but serving God from our
hearts, because He alone has every claim upon
our service, and from Him alone can creatures
derive any claim upon it. He has a first claim
to our all, our whole effort and our whole time;
there can be no lawful break in His service, but
even when rest be needed we must still keep
His service before us therein, not looking upon
a holiday as a reward, but only as a means.

THE RULE OF LIFE. It is evident that
this choice of the greater good is a perfection
offered to all. 'Be you perfect', says Our Lord,
'as also your heavenly Father is perfect' (Matt.
V, 48); none can say that He does not bid them
be perfect. That the counsels are in a true sense
proposed to all and possible for all is the doctrine of Saint Thomas and the Fathers; but this
is a point that need not be discussed further here.
At least it is true that religious are peculiarly
bound to the practice of perfection; in what
sense, we may briefly consider. The perfection
of anything consists in the attainment of its end,
and the end of man, we have seen, is God, to
whom, indeed, he fully attains only in the next
world. But it is by sanctifying grace and supernatural charity that he attains to God, so far as
he may while here below, and it is therefore the

more abundant possession of these that makes him more perfect. The chief and universal hindrances to this grace and charity are the lust of the flesh, the lust of the eyes, or the desire of riches, and the pride of life, or the desire of honour. These every man must combat who is seriously striving after perfection. But religious have taken upon themselves this combat in a peculiarly vigorous form. The vows which they take are directly aimed at these hindrances. They take upon themselves permanent obligations, obligations under sin which otherwise would not exist for them, as a direct means of overcoming these obstacles to their own perfection. By poverty they renounce riches, by chastity they renounce the flesh, by obedience they renounce themselves.

It follows that when a religious is trying to order his life to God's greater service, the first thing he must look to after the commandments, are his vows. It is these which make him what he is. They constitute in an especial sense the duties of his calling. And from their very nature it is clear that, if he be faithfully observing them, nothing can be very wrong with him, because, with God's help, he is dealing successfully with the foes that are most to be feared. The vows will be considered individually later in the retreat, but some attempt to consider their scope and how we are observing them will not be out of

place here. Yet they are far from exhausting
our knowledge of God's will in our regard. Vows
are common to all religious; but the rule of the
particular order to which they have been called,
sanctioned as it is by the Church, is also the expression of God's will in their regard. And there
is also the living voice, the superiors, to whom
obedience is due. To them it belongs, within
proper limits, to direct our lives, and to give an
authoritative decision in case of doubt. Thus we
have ample guidance, and we can never truly say
that we do not know what God would have of us.

DELUSIONS. It all seems so simple. It all
really is simple; only there is a constant danger
of illusion, because these principles are of such
universal application and of such compelling force.
We must not think that illusions are to be found
only among the mentally defective, or at most
in a few whose fervour has turned to fanaticism.
We are all subject to delusions, otherwise we
should all be saints. Only the saints have been
truly rational; only they have not only assented
to the great truths of that faith to which reason
leads us, but have carried them through. But
from that reasonable service poor human nature
is ever shrinking, and any little excuse is enough
to blind us, because we have not the courage
to take a careful look into it. There are, of
course, some more pretentious deceits. Some
sort of a divine call, for instance, there may be

to one work or another; but it can never run counter to obedience, rather perfect obedience and readiness for all else is the very test and stamp of a true call. But every-day delusions are of a less dramatic and more contemptible kind.

Again and again it must be said, nothing can be too great, and nothing too small, to be conformed to God's holy Will. If we are to put real meaning into our lives, we must not live in the vague, *dans l'à peu près,* but must ever be bringing our life from day to day, nay, from hour to hour and minute to minute, to this touch-stone. Our actual abode, and the others who are to dwell with us there, including our superiors: the outward conditions of our lives, such as our food, our clothing, the room, if such it be, assigned to us: our success in work or prayer, given that we on our side have done all that in us lies: our intercourse with our relations and others, including visits and correspondence: our health, apart, that is, from blameworthy carelessness, our good name, the nature of our work — nothing save sin can be excluded from the list of things towards which we must practise a true indifference, as explained above, so that we have our inclinations and passions under effective control, and with gaze serene and clear only need to be shown the will of God to recognise it easily and accomplish it with all our might.

Would that we could indeed be rid of all illusion and self-deceit! This would mean perfect peace, perfect freedom, perfect holiness. It would also mean apostolic power. Indifference is no placid inefficiency; on the contrary, taken with the accompanying quest for perfection, which alone explains it, it spells success all along the line. With such a generous spirit at work there can be no storms of the dangerous kind, because no sacrifice can be too hard. There is nothing like it for oiling the wheels; the truly obedient can have no difficulties with superiors, and a pure intention means disinterested charity and peace with all. None the less, tremendous energy is there, tremendous courage and endurance, and a vast supply of grace.

THIRD DAY.

SIN.

PATRON: St. Mary Magdalen.

READING: Mark XIII; Epistle to Philemon; Imitation I, 23-24.

FIRST MEDITATION: The Three Sins (The Angels' Sin, Adam's Sin, A single Sin, The Crucifix).

SECOND MEDITATION: The Tale of Sins (The Tale of Sins, Sin and the Sinner, God, Prayer).

CONSIDERATION: Prayer (General Principles, Mental Prayer).

THIRD MEDITATION: Hell (Faith and Reason, The Motive of Fear, The Punishment).

✠

ADVENT.

Drear it is,
  Tree and plant are shorn,
And earth, her splendour by the chilly wind
    Scattered and torn
Dons mistier cloak to screen the woe behind.

Drearier yet,
  As though all-baleful sin
Heaven's quickening fires, and field and flower could numb;
    Till Thou within
Supplant the voice of nature that is dumb:

Till Thou come down,
  Shaking off every frost,
O winter glory of the midnight cave,
    And all we lost
Hail with fresh hope the mighty one to save!

THIRD DAY, FIRST MEDITATION:

THE THREE SINS.

IT is not improbable, it is even to be hoped, that during our meditations upon the end of man, however captivating we may have found the ideal held before us, we yet had a lurking conviction that it was worlds away from being a picture of our actual lives. And now we must begin to set things right. We must understand what it is to miss our end, to commit sin. We turn now to the reverse side, as it were, of our meditation on the end of man, and seek to understand that it is sin alone that can and does stand in the way of our attaining it. The righteous judgment of God, the world's history, our own reason, all declare the hideous folly and wickedness of sin. And as sin is founded on pride, so the undoing of sin must begin from a feeling of shame and humiliation at our own guilt. In order to bring home to ourselves a sense of our own degradation, we may imagine our soul imprisoned, as it were, in this corruptible body, the nobler and stronger element, that is, confined and held fast by the meaner; and our whole self we may picture in exile in this vale of tears, thrust forth among the beasts, cast out by God and man, like the scape-goat of old, as a thing unclean and sinful. In abandoning our Maker we have abandoned truth and righteousness,

besmirched our intellect and will, and forfeited
our manhood.

We beg that we may indeed feel shame and
confusion, because for a single mortal sin so many
have been damned, and we have so often deserved
to be damned on account of our many sins. If
we are not conscious of having committed mortal
sins, we have great reason to thank the Divine
Mercy; but we still have many sins of which to
be ashamed. 'If we say that we have not sin,
we deceive ourselves, and the truth is not in us'
(1 John 1, 8). We may contrast these many sins
with the isolated sins which we are about to
consider, and reflect that through our carelessness
and tepidity we have again and again deserved
to be cast off by God, and to be allowed to
go our own mad way along the road to everlasting ruin.

THE ANGELS' SIN. It may at once be
admitted that about the angels' fall we know
very little. But the one or two points which
theology puts beyond reasonable doubt yield
matter enough for thought. In the first place,
they were pure spirits, Satan doubtless the noblest
and mightiest of them. They were created in
grace, destined for the beatific vision, and given
all proper means thereunto. But there was first
to be some sort of probation; some service and
obedience to their Maker was required of them.
Some suppose that the Incarnation was made

known to them, and that they were called upon
to adore their Lord and God in a nature so
inferior to their own. But no positive certainty
attaches to conjectures of this kind, where Scripture and Tradition give little or no help. Beyond
question there was a probation of some kind,
in which a large number abused their free-will,
withheld the obedience due to the Divine Majesty,
and in a moment were hurled into a place of
torment, no less swiftly created for them, and
were in some mysterious way subjected to the
fire thereof.

Their sin was very great, both because of
their clearer knowledge and the comparative
absence of temptation. Yet the terrific punishment
that fell upon it is staggering enough. God did
not spare His own fair handiwork, but decreed an
eternity of dreadful pain, and still more dreadful
banishment from His own presence. He made
an arch-enemy to Himself, the leader of that rebel
array, who should go about with his attendant
fiends marring the divine scheme. There was no
second chance; this single mortal sin, committed
and punished, may be, in the twinkling of an eye,
made all the difference. And so we come to
ourselves. How if even upon our first transgression, the first impudent 'I will not serve',
He had taken us at our word, and measured
His strength against ours, if He had condemned
us at once and for ever! Could He be afraid

to punish us? Let us humble ourselves beneath
His powerful hand, confess His power, and our
guilt, marvel that He has borne with us so long,
and be filled with confusion at our reckless
wrong-doing. This very shame and confusion,
as profitable to us as it is acceptable to Him,
we crave of His mercy.

ADAM'S SIN. Of Adam's sin we know far
more, by reason of its great significance for the
doctrine of original sin and grace. Like the
angels, Adam and Eve set out from a far better
state than that in which we find ourselves. They
were in sanctifying grace, free from the revolt
of lower tendencies against the higher, free also
from death, which was only threatened as a
punishment in case of transgression. Not that
this better state was in any way due to them;
it was not demanded, it was not attainable, by
their nature as such. It would not have been
in any way contrary to God's goodness or wisdom
to have created them without these privileges;
otherwise it would have been equally contrary
to them to deprive them of the same. Concupiscence, death, ignorance, all our other weaknesses might have been theirs, without grace and
without the prospect of the beatific vision. Their
final end, to be attained fully only after death,
would have been a derived and merely natural
knowledge of God, which yet would have satisfied all their desires. And in place of super-

natural gifts and graces they would have had special helps, also of a merely natural kind, to enable them to keep the natural law and attain to that end. But the Divine Goodness was thus lavish towards them; yet they, too, were to have a trial, before being awarded unending bliss. And now Satan began his depredations on the human race. Fitly enough, the tempter's tool was the serpent, which stealthily glides along, till with a savage, sudden stroke it brings death; such was the beast that by God's curse was evermore to portray Satan, with a new meaning given to his gait and his enmity with man. Not, of course, that we need suppose that the serpent's own organs actually produced human speech, but Satan could make his words to issue from its mouth. And Eve dallied with the temptation; when she had sinned, her first thought was that her consort should sin too, and her cajoling prevailed.

When Adam sinned, he sinned in his divinely-given capacity of head of the race, and what he lost, he lost for the race. The history of the ages and the tragedy of every human soul is summed up in that one sin. From him all inherit death, the lust of the flesh, and that privation of grace, that stain, that inherited guilt, which we call original sin; not a guilt that of itself is enough to plunge us into hell-fire, but which excludes from the vision of God. Only

Our Lord and His Blessed Mother were exempt from original sin and concupiscence. The rest of mankind are like the children of a dethroned king, who in him have forfeited their royal rights. This inherited stain the waters of baptism wipe out; not, however, concupiscence. To understand what concupiscence has meant, one has but to take a glance at history. Why have things gone wrong? It is always the same story, the same thirst after sensual pleasures, after money, after revenge, after all that is inordinate. How little men have known that indifference, that purity of intention, which is the only reasonable attitude of man! And what devastation has followed!

We perhaps think ourselves safely ensconced in our paradise. But we have far less reason to feel secure than Satan or Adam. And our punishment, swift and sharp, would be far less astonishing than theirs. Do we not see how perilous has been our weakness?

A SINGLE SIN. Lastly, to bring the matter yet more home to ourselves, we meditate upon the case of a man condemned to hell for a single mortal sin. That any man has been so condemned is, of course, only a hypothesis; yet not a hypothesis to be rejected lightly. To rush to the conclusion that such a thing can never have happened, is to misunderstand the nature of mortal sin. If it did not deserve, and thoroughly deserve, an eternity of hell-fire, it would not be mortal sin. Was God bound to put off the reckoning, to await repentance or further sin? We may think of many ways in which a soul may have come to commit one mortal sin, and thereupon be called to judgment. It will be well to picture a way not too unlike what appears to be the possible road to perdition for ourselves. To every soul, as has been said, there is one road easier than all others. And how far have we sauntered carelessly along it?

THE CRUCIFIX. We have been spared. And therefore our last word is with our crucified Saviour. Our meditation upon the three sins has filled us with confusion at our own reckless folly, but we dare not stop there. Such thoughts are too crushing for our timid souls to be taken alone. They need a good recovery, a quick return to a deepened confidence in God, and to livelier generosity towards Him. We gaze upon our crucifix, therefore, and ask our Redeemer what there was that could allure Him, Creator as He was, to empty Himself, to take the form of a servant, to suffer a dreadful passion and death — what, save ingratitude and sordid guilt? And we turn to ourselves. How have we on our side dealt with Christ? Ah, that is now but too clear, we scarce can bear to think of it. What are we doing for Christ now? Are we making earnest endeavour to atone for the past, to order our lives henceforth aright, to reap the full benefit of these spiritual exercises? And the future? As we see Him there, His cross a pledge of forgiveness, of love, of desire, it seems but a little thing to suffer something in return, to be ready to bear our own cross for Him, should His greater service so demand. It remains but to cast ourselves upon His boundless love, to solicit the help without which no effort can avail.

THIRD DAY, SECOND MEDITATION:

THE TALE OF SINS.

We eagerly defend, and indeed glorify our past, glorify it perhaps more than the truth allows. Let us now deliberately recognise that we have committed both faults and follies, in thought, word and deed. Mere follies are not dwelt on for their own sake; yet to force ourselves to face them may shake a self-complacency not a little, and our ardour of self-adulation, and thus we may be prepared in spirit for the spectacle of real faults. We are now to look ourselves and our own sins squarely in the face. It is not a pleasant spectacle that meets our eye, but a necessary and a profitable one. Thus alone can we attain to a deep and practical contrition, which is our present object, and incidentally we lay the true foundation of humility, which is the profound knowledge of ourselves and of our own shortcomings. It is our moral disorders that chiefly come into consideration, and the abandonment of our own ideals.

We may help ourselves with the same mental picture as in the last meditation. We pray for the grace of profound sorrow for our sins. We can never bewail them too much, even though they should be but venial. The sorrow of an Aloysius, let us say, for the sins of his past life may perhaps seem to us to be exaggerated, to verge on the ridiculous; but it is we who err, not the saints. Where there is real sin, there is always matter for intense grief. It is important that we should understand this, nay, that we should feel the grief. We pray very earnestly that we may both understand and grieve.

THE TALE OF SINS. To attain this object, we institute a review of our own sins, both to discover and to realise them; that is to say, we proceed at once to a general survey of our lives, to examine what these sins are, and afterwards we shall try to awaken within ourselves a clearer sense of their malice. We should consider them as though till now we had done nothing to expiate them, in order to see, not what through the Divine Mercy we may actually have become, but what through our own fault we should have made of ourselves. The former, so far as there is no disorder therein, is from God, the latter all from ourselves. Again, we shall not estimate

accurately the number and species of our sins,
as though for a general confession. As a matter
of fact this meditation is a useful preliminary to
a general confession; but for the present we had
best put all idea of the latter out of our heads;
it will come up for consideration later on in the
day. Now it is only a summary view that is
required. Some sort of division of our lives is
useful; the obvious one is that according to time;
for example, the period before our entry into
the order, and the several stages of our religious
life. In each of these we consider what were
our chief faults, or rather series of faults; an
isolated sin may stand out here and there, but
in general it is better to insist rather on the
habit or weakness of which they are the outcome,
for we thus see them in their true historical
setting, and advance in self-knowledge. Our chief
dangers remain ever the same. In an annual
retreat, however, it is not necessary always to
run over the whole of our lives. Usually it will
be enough to run over the offences of the past
year, with or without divisions of time, place or
the like to help us. Some prominent sins or
series of sins may then be added from the previous
time, well remembered from similar meditations
or general confessions. Once more it must be
remarked that the vows contain what is most
fundamental; and in general it is evident that the
account of ourselves which we try to give either

to ourselves or to another, as sketched in the last consideration, must of necessity indicate our chief failings.

SIN AND THE SINNER. We now make earnest endeavour to realise the foulness and malice of sin. It is true that one must distinguish what is forbidden because it is evil, as blasphemy or theft, and what is evil because it is forbidden, as eating meat on Fridays. Nevertheless the general object of precepts of the latter kind is either to determine an obligation already existing in the vague, such as that of mortification, or, in the case of the vows and other obligations of religious, to urge the practice of perfection. Given such precepts, it is only unreason and disordered passion that can refuse obedience.

Even if we are confining ourselves in the main to the faults of the year, we should make a strong effort to convince ourselves that they are in themselves contemptible, and that we are contemptible for having committed them. Not merely our sins, but our ordinary defects should be branded too. *Parturiunt montes*: we, who have so solemnly consecrated ourselves to God, and in all that is most essential have renounced our own will and pleasure, how swiftly we pass from the sublime to the unworthy and ridiculous, when we greedily gather up crumbs there where we have abjured the banquet! Are we aping the rich, when not a penny can pass through our

6 *

hands save by the will of another? Do we preach
self-mastery, and celebrate the event with good
cheer? And if anything can make obedience igno-
minious, it is to forget Him for whose sake and
whom always we must obey, and to see nothing
in a superior but a poor mortal like ourselves.

And so we run through the list, ever trying
to bring home to ourselves all that is mean,
despicable, wrong in the sins to which we find
ourselves most subject. 'Lord, that I may see!'
We must also consider our whole state, whether
perhaps we have been on the down grade, whether
we have been hardening ourselves in imperfections
or even sin, whether, in a word, we have been
lapsing into tepidity. Such a state of affairs is
more dangerous than any individual sin, because
it means the loss of ideals, the loss of generosity,
the loss, if we are not careful, of all facility in
repentance. It needs a great effort to shake off
this torpor; we can begin it here, but we shall
need to consummate it in the Sacred Heart of
Jesus, later in the retreat.

When we have considered the sins in themselves,
and even our defects, we try to throw fresh light
upon them from without. I have sinned against
God. I have endeavoured to understand more
clearly what is sin. And now, who am I? Who
is God?

Who am I? After all, we are not so very
important. Even in the house in which we live,

our disappearance would not bring matters to a
standstill.   Somebody else would soon appear
to take up our work, and perhaps do it better.
What, then, if we consider ourselves in comparison
with our whole order, our whole country — the
Church — the world?   Of what possible account
are we?   What is even all mankind, compared
to all the angels and saints in heaven?   What,
either in number, knowledge, happiness or glory?
Those blessed spirits see enough to move their
compassion, but not any very profound admiration.
What do they think, for instance, of these elaborate
preparations for mutual annihilation by the 'advanced' races, by hundreds of thousands who
at the selected moment will doubtless be bam-
boozled into thirsting for each other's blood,
but certainly will have very little idea as to why
they were set to do this? [1]   But trifles of this
sort scarcely call for attention in the presence
of so much that is directly and essentially evil.
But what are all things created compared to the
Creator?   We have seen it, they are nothing,
less than nothing, absolutely subject to His sway,
their very existence depending on His good pleasure.   Myself, then, and Almighty God?

What indeed am I, body and soul?   Even in
my body there is death, and the foreshadowing
of death; and what can I behold in my soul,

---

[1] Written originally before the War.

apart from the merciful healing of God's grace, but a kind of running sore, ever pouring out fault upon fault and sin upon sin, all that poisonous matter to whose presence I am slowly awaking?

GOD. I have sinned against God. It is a matter between myself and God. I may use other creatures to help me to understand my insignificance; but it is not with them that I have to do. Myself against God! Myself, such a creature as I have seen, committing these dreadful offences against God! Who then is God? This too we have considered. It is ignorance, stupidity, blindness against infinite Wisdom; weakness, instability, nothingness against Omnipotence; iniquity against the Fount of all justice and holiness; malice and perversity against perfect Goodness. How shall we understand what it is, to offend God? We should need first of all to sound the depths of our own worthlessness; and even if that were light and easy, the Divine Essence remains incomprehensible to all created intellect. Any notion that we can form of God still leaves His beauty and goodness and uttermost perfection for the more part beyond our ken. Yet according as we can form a clearer idea of God upon the one hand, and of ourselves upon the other, the clearer will be our idea of sin, and the more vivid our horror.

We may advert also to God's creatures. How could the holy angels, the sword of the Divine

Justice, still bear with us, watch over us, and, with the saints, pray for us? How could earth and sky and beast still serve us? With all these we have been out of joint, we have gone our own wilful way, perverting all beneath us, neglecting all above us. All were ready to help us, all did help us, but we would have none of it. We have been a blot upon their perfect service. Rightly, then, they might take vengeance on us, the whole court of Heaven above, all nature below. And we can think of our fellow-men, of the scandal which we have given, of all the good we have omitted to do them. They too have ample reason for complaint. And we have failed to profit from so much that was good in them.

PRAYER. But, once more, all is not to end in terror and crushing pain. We cannot convince ourselves too forcibly of the heinousness of our sins, and therefore, after the meditation upon the three sins had stirred up shame and confusion in us, we passed to a more particular consideration of our own sins, and have sought by every means to awaken a detestation and horror of them. But now at the end we must remember that God's mercy has been greater than the multitude of our sins, and, as with the prodigal, it is trust in our Father which must prevail. We have no claims to urge, nothing but evil to confess, evil for all His benefits; but

we extol His mercy in still preserving us alive,
for bringing us once more before Him, for all
the graces which He has given us, and is still
ready to give us. Such a welling source of
goodness we will love, and, because we love,
we will grieve yet more heartily for our sins,
and resolve, trusting in this boundless mercy,
to live far otherwise in the future.

THIRD DAY, CONSIDERATION:

PRAYER.

It is not uncommon to hear religious orders
distinguished as active and contemplative; a division which at the best may easily mislead. Contemplation, properly so called, is a form of mental
prayer, and anybody may practise it. The so-
called active orders all practise it, and sometimes
more than the so-called contemplative orders,
which are sometimes more addicted to vocal
prayer, that is, to the singing of the Office and
the like. This is not a topic that calls for further
discussion here; but what should be noticed is
this, that every order or congregation must to
some extent be contemplative. It must train its
members to mental prayer, so necessary an exercise in the quest of perfection, and it must not
on any account suffer them to lose themselves
in external activity, to the detriment of the spirit
of inward recollection and union with God. Nor

should any religious allow himself to be permanently overwhelmed with work or business; like our Blessed Lord, he should at times hurry back to more intimate union with God, even though all be clamouring for him. This union with God is his first and supreme duty and nothing can excuse him from it. Nor indeed can anything replace it. Active work may absorb his interest for a while; but not for ever; sooner or later he must fall back for support upon his prayer, and either find it there or succumb.

Prayer, then, is of two kinds, vocal and mental. It is of the essence of vocal prayer as here understood, not that there should be any physical utterance, though this may also be, but that a fixed form of words should be followed. It is our thoughts which follow the words, not words that follow our thoughts. We endeavour to conform our sentiments to an already existing prayer, which we are reciting, either aloud or to ourselves. But mental prayer consists of serious reflection upon the truths of our faith, with a view to ordering our lives in accordance with them. It is our own innermost soul which we are stirring up and pouring out. Of the higher sorts of mental prayer, wherein the initiative lies with God rather than with the human soul, we do not propose to treat here. Directors of souls will find it useful to have read Père Poulain's *Graces of Interior Prayer (Grâces d' Oraison),* and some mystic treatises by the saints themselves, such as Saint Teresa's works, and most of all her *Way of Perfection*; all may find it a help to understand that God is wonderful in His saints, but there is some danger of delusion if they come to look upon ecstatic conditions as practical politics for them, for such favours are given but rarely, and to very mortified souls. Only they should not be afraid if by degrees a single thought or topic comes to be easier and more engrossing for them than intellectual discourse; there is nothing wrong or even very abnormal about that, but they should explain the state of affairs to their director. This is not very likely to be an early development in the spiritual life; still, we cannot bind Almighty God by human rules.

GENERAL PRINCIPLES. In the first place, we must not make the distinction between vocal and mental prayer too sharp a one. On the contrary, it is an excellent thing to mingle them together. It may often be a great help in mental prayer, when for some reason or another things are not going well, to recite fervently some familiar vocal prayer, even though it be but an ejaculation. And on the other hand, it may put more life into vocal prayer if we can stop for a while and think more carefully of what we are saying, put more meaning into it, and fervour. Moreover there are intermediate stages in prayer, which pave the way from the purely vocal to the purely mental. They chiefly consist in a slow and reflective recitation of vocal prayers; but we may also attempt a cleansing of the heart through a detailed consideration of the commandments, the seven deadly sins or the like, with a view to discovering faults and imperfections. Virtues may be considered in the same way, or our rules, which for us are the manifestation of God's will.

For all prayer a certain amount of preparation is needed, whereof one of the most important features is recollection. This is needed at the commencement of the prayer itself. To attempt to plunge suddenly into it when our mind is full of other things, and perhaps even our body is not yet in a suitable posture, is an act of irreverence and neglect. Before we begin — before we kneel down, if possible — we should think of what we are about to do. To laugh and talk, for instance, right up to the chapel door, is to make practically certain that we enter God's house in an improper frame of mind. But with a religious, recollection should be habitual. Habits of dissipation and frivolity are peculiarly fatal to prayer. It should not need a violent wrench to recall us to the Divine Presence. The only way to pray well is to pray always. If our ordinary trend of thought is on a different plane from what is required in prayer, we cannot be surprised if we find prayer difficult. But the religious who is inwardly and outwardly devout and recollected comes to look at everything more and more in God, and to pass easily from creature to Creator. There is action and reaction; fervent and frequent prayer itself brings it about that thoughts of God and spiritual things become as it were part and parcel of our minds, and the leading factor in our mental attitude. If the river be very full it must needs overflow; and prayer knows no barriers of time and place. Still, even if distractions should be very persistent, we must not lose heart. No doubt we are not perfect in our intercourse with God, any more than in our intercourse with our fellow-creatures; but it is the same charity that urges us to both, and it is worth while risking minor offences — more worth while with God, who also is quicker to understand and pardon, because He knows all.

For prayer there is, besides, no small need of mortification. The two go hand in hand. Prayer means a stern control of mind and body. It means a severance from all that is most present to both, and they will be restless enough till trained to obey. The body must be quiet and give as little trouble as may be; the mind must be working, but it is upon matter which is not of a nature to make a vivid impression except at the cost of effort.

Effort there must be, yet there is also a sense in which we should be restful. Just as we should

not hurry into it, so we should not hurry on
when we have commenced it. When it is a case
of any kind of liturgical or public prayer, there
may be irreverence in delay, though the greater
danger of irreverence lies in undue haste; but
at other times we should avoid making it a duty
and preoccupation to 'finish', or to arrive at any
particular point, when there is really no such
duty upon us. It is the attempt to save time
that really loses it; no progress is made, and
a tired head is the only certain result. The end
of prayer is not to pass a number of thoughts
through the mind, nor to formulate a certain
number of petitions. It is to enlighten the understanding and enkindle the will, or rather to
prepare the way for this, should God so will.
When, therefore, this object is being secured,
there is no possible reason for bustling on, but
rather no particle of the gift at hand should be
allowed to escape, and the holy thought should
be cherished and allowed to sink in, we should
abandon ourselves to it without care, the will
should be allowed to pour out all its desire
or joy.

One more point. It is summed up in the
words: 'Ask, and you shall receive'. There is
not a land inside Europe or out of it that has
not crying need of most earnest and efficacious
prayer; and blessed is he who takes the need
to heart. And all about us we see much that

demands our best prayer. We should pray for
what is thus wholly good, not because we ought
to pray for it, but because it is our duty to
secure it. It is this latter spirit which springs
from vivid faith, and does violence to Heaven.

MENTAL PRAYER. Vocal prayer has the advantage that it is easy for all, and that it is
a lesson in sound doctrine and a sound form of
words. The more any prayer has the official
sanction of the Church, such as those used in
the liturgy, the more we should value it. Prayers
composed by those since canonised are also to
be much esteemed, because the mouth speaks
out of the abundance of the heart, and their
heart was right before God. But in the religious
life, and indeed in any serious quest of holiness,
mental prayer must play a very large part. It is
chiefly of two kinds, meditation and contemplation.
In the former it is reasoning that predominates,
it is some truth that is the more immediate object of our thought, so that the prayer is rather
more abstract in character; the latter presents
some visible scene or event to our view, we hear
and see concrete persons, and most of all our
Lord. Contemplation, it stands to reason, is the
easier, because there is more room for senses
and imagination, and more play of the affections.
It is usually better, therefore, to let this be one's
normal form of mental prayer, to make oneself
familiar with the life of our Blessed Lord, not

merely as it is presented in books of meditation, but most of all in the gospels, and to live His life once more, uniting our own thereto. We cannot be too interested in our Divine Master, nor penetrate too intimately into His life, so far as the evidence allows us. In this way most easily we shall come to be like Him, or rather He will take fullest possession of us, that we may live and act entirely according to His mind, that our every thought and word and deed may be rather His than ours. This His grace can accomplish; and every little effort or aspiration of ours will receive from Him a more than generous response. Meanwhile there is a certain drill necessary in mental prayer, not to be despised, teaching us the careful preparation and beginning, and the wide range possible in the body of the prayer; it is freedom, but to be profitable must be ordered freedom. Abstract speculation is never to be pursued for its own sake, it is the will that matters. The value of mental prayer lies in its working truths and principles into the very fabric of our souls, in a way that set prayers do not. We are also free to make resolutions which are really practical, and to devise sure means of carrying our purposes into effect.

Memory, understanding and will; these are to recall the subject-matter of our prayer, examine it, digest it, make it of practical effect for ourselves. These three should work well together; it is good

often to be interjecting direct and fervent prayers,
but our soul needs a sure foundation of reasoned
truth or vivid example if it is to be deeply moved.
We must be prepared for many a dry prayer,
and must be patient; yet we must not acquiesce
in a dead-and-alive sort of meditation week after
week, but must pull ourselves together, and
examine whether our own laziness be at fault,
whether our method be correct, or whether perhaps there be some physical cause at work, such
as bad health or want of sleep. Sometimes a
little variety is enough to set things going again,
for example, a larger proportion of vocal prayer.
We must not easily flatter ourselves that God is
making trial of us. One prayer is always good —
'Lord, teach us to pray.'

THIRD DAY, THIRD MEDITATION:

HELL.

From shame we came to sorrow, from sorrow
to a firm purpose never to sin again. And this
purpose is clinched by the contemplation of Hell.
More generous motives for the avoidance of sin
will appear as the retreat proceeds, and have
in part appeared already; yet, weak creatures
that we are, we cannot understand too clearly
whither it brings us, nor thank the Divine Goodness sufficiently that it has not brought us thither
already. This contemplation of Hell helps much

to put us into the right frame of mind. We
learn to be humble and distrust ourselves, to
trust only in our heavenly Father. We are but
brands which He has plucked from the burning;
we deserve to be cast once more upon the flames.

FAITH AND REASON. Hell is a fact. It was
not discovered by an enterprising explorer. It
does not admit of ocular demonstration. Nevertheless the divine message vouches for its being
a fact. It was said above that in the matter of
riches Our Lord was something of an alarmist.
Much more does this hold of Hell. Writers of
various schools sometimes leave out such traits.
They fashion a Christ after their own liking,
and not after the four gospels. He is all sweetness
and mildness; but of the terrible earnestness with
which He sought to push home certain momentous
and disquieting truths we hear little or nothing.
Yet so it was. On Hell He laid tremendous
emphasis. If our right eye be a cause of sin
to us, we are to pluck it out and cast it from
us, and so of our right hand; better far to lose
a limb, than with it to be thrown into Hell
(Matth. V, 29, 30), into everlasting punishment,
everlasting fire (Matth. XXV, 41, 46).

Lasciate ogni speranza! They are there till
they pay the whole debt, and the whole debt
can never be paid. It is at best a hard saying,
but all the more so for the sickly sentimentality
of our own age. We could not have divined

merely from the consideration of mortal sin itself
that it deserved such a penalty, nor after the
revelation do we fully understand it. Hell, therefore, remains something of a mystery. On the
other hand it is also plain that the great difficulty
which many find in the doctrine is due to their
own unhealthy outlook, to an excessive horror
of pain, and an all too slight horror of moral
evil. They would like to muddle through life
just anyhow, with a comfortable feeling that all
will be right in the end. But will it? And are
they really so comfortable? In any case it is
plain how degrading are these pseudo-humane
views, how derogatory to man's true dignity.
All significance and worth is taken out of his
existence, and from a child of God and heir of
the Kingdom he becomes, like the beasts, the
creature of a day, blindly seeking to get off as
cheap as he can. And how helpless is such a
policy before the stern facts of life! It abolishes
Christian fortitude; the cross remains, and it is
a bitter and irremediable cross, because it is not
the cross of Christ. Men banish Hell from their
sight, and rivet their eyes upon the things of
this world; but Heaven is lost to view also.

The cure is to understand better the nature
of mortal sin, and the infinite majesty and holiness of God. Mortal sin is an outrage for
which no sufficient penalty can be paid. It is in
a manner an infinite outrage, by reason of the

infinite distance between man and God, as though
a worthless fellow had contemned the best and
greatest of monarchs. It is the very consummation
of reckless impudence and despicable crime. Almighty God has consequently a right to a punishment which shall in a manner be infinite; not
in its severity, which varies with the sin, and
moreover is generally believed to be less than
a rigorous justice would warrant, but in its
duration. The same tremendous guilt for which
no effort of man could atone, till the heavens
opened and the Second Person of the Blessed
Trinity took flesh, to live and die for us, remains
unredeemed in them who have refused His saving grace. Justice does not suffer that they be
put on a par with the saints, that virgin and
harlot, devil and apostle, martyr and persecutor
should all be as one. If all are to attain in the
end to the blessed vision of God, what matters
it if they eat and drink and abandon themselves
to all vices, seeing that in comparison of eternity
a thousand years are but a day? And so we
are brought to the flat opposite of that word
of the Son of Sirach, that if we remember what
is to befall us last, we shall never sin (Ecclus.
VII, 40).

THE MOTIVE OF FEAR. Our prayer is that
we may have an intense realisation of the pains
which the damned suffer, so that, if ever through
our own fault we should become insensible to

7 *

divine love — perfect love casteth out fear — at least the fear of punishment may keep us from falling into sin.

It is a reasonable fear for which we ask. None but a madman is free from all fear; and the one wholly reasonable fear is the fear of being severed from God, the fear of sin and Hell. It is but a childish boast, and even the forswearing of the noblest part of our being, to pretend to have no fear of what lies beyond our sense. We are not speaking of merely emotional fear, of the sudden start or the pale cheek; these are largely beyond our control, and may be due to fact or delusion. But we may have a deliberate and intense conviction that there is an evil which may come upon us unless we are careful to avoid it, an evil so great that it is reasonable to be at utmost pain to avoid it. Such should be our fear of Hell.

This fear is also necessary, necessary to a proper understanding of sin and of ourselves, and without it our concept of God himself would not only be inadequate but incorrect. Only a vivid impression of those dreadful pains can give us some idea of the foulness of the guilt that deserves them, and of the justice and power and holiness of Him who inflicts them. And we come to know ourselves, to be more alive to the evil inclinations and sins that would hurry us to our doom, and to mistrust our own strength.

Lastly, this fear is holy. Of this there can be no doubt, seeing that Our Lord has so strongly exhorted us to it. Nor have the saints ever made light of it. It is a creature which eminently deserves to be used, because it can help us so much to know, love and serve God. To know Him, as we have explained above. To love Him; for as a boy cannot really be friends with the master who cannot keep him in order, because the element of respect is lacking, so it is not a weak 'good-natured' God that could secure our love, one that should always, as it were, be giving in to us, indulging our every weakness, and never exacting peremptorily that His command should be obeyed. As it is, we understand that we cannot afford to take liberties with Him, that if in His infinite goodness He creates man and offers him everlasting bliss, it is not to become the laughing-stock of His own creatures. No; it is His will which ever prevails, though He leaves it to us to choose between His mercy and His justice, our glory and our chastisement. He has no need of aught created; if we are mad enough to disobey, He suffers nothing by our sin or by our punishment. And thus we come to understand what is the Divine Mercy, because we see how entirely unnecessary and, if we may use the word, how disinterested have been our Heavenly Father's efforts to save us. It is the same God who

threatens us with Hell, and who lightens our
way to Heaven, terrific even in His love; we
cannot comprehend His infinite condescension
except we acknowledge His supreme justice,
and according to the measure of our fear will
be our love. It is the sight of the abyss that
sends us back to our Father's side, knowing
well that He alone can and will save us from
His own chastisements.

And what helps us to know and love God,
will also help us to serve Him. We know the
frail stuff of which we are made; if now and
again a warmer breath of charity passes over
our cold hearts, that can but make us all the
more ready to humble ourselves, to submit to
be terrified by Hell, rather than to run any risk
of offending so good a God. For the bright
sunshine does not last for ever; a dark hour
may come, when our Heavenly Father may seem
far away, and the Devil, the world and the flesh
may seem fair enough to our altered gaze, and
in that hour we must be armed with sterner
thoughts if we are to stand. We pray, therefore, and we pray rightly, for an intense realisation of the pains which the damned suffer, as
for a great mercy and a sovereign safeguard,
and we do all that in us lies to attain it.

THE PUNISHMENT. We may imagine, then,
a great dungeon, or a lake of fire, in thick
darkness. It is much the safer doctrine to hold

that the fire of Hell is a literal and material fire; but about the mode of its action many questions may be raised, which need not here detain us. God is almighty, and can fulfil His purposes in more ways than we can think of. We call in our imagination to help us, knowing that at least we cannot exaggerate the total effect. We see dreadful sights, fires, fires preying upon human souls, perhaps by the latter feeling all the sensations of burning bodies; we see countenances distorted by pain. We may reflect upon sins of sight, of evil pictures and evil literature, spread abroad for the havoc of souls. We may consider our own faults in the use of our eyes. We hear wails, cries, blasphemies. 'We fools!' (Ecclus. v, 4.) However clever the politician, however brave the soldier or sailor, however successful the merchant, still, if it all end in Hell, his verdict on his own life will be, that he was a fool. And even though they write his life in several volumes, and erect a statue to him, and collect money for a foundation in his honour, that verdict will still remain unshaken, because it is embedded with the man himself in those everlasting flames. How many of them thought the religious life folly! And how many would now see in it a sane and welcome precaution, could they live their life again! All the greater is the folly of them that do not use it aright.

The religious must be especially careful against offending in speech. Smell is the sense of luxury, which only wealth and leisure can study to please. In the hovels of Christ's poor there is still to be found a foulness of food and air and clothing which may be our best safeguard against the stench and unutterable corruption of Hell. Lastly, there is the excruciating pain of touch, the pain of burning. And greater than these pains of sense is the pain of loss, the pain of the soul that against its inward yearning for its only rest apprehends God as a being to be shunned, feared, hated, because of intolerable guilt.

In conclusion we think of the souls that perished before and after Christ, and during His life, and thank Him that we are not of any of these; and think of all His love and mercy.

FOURTH DAY.

BETHLEHEM.

PATRON: St. Joseph.

READING: Ephesians I-III; Apoc. IV-V; Imitation II, 7·8.

FIRST MEDITATION: Death and Judgment (Death, The Particular Judgment, The Last Judgment).

SECOND MEDITATION: Christ the King (The New Foundation, The Call, Greater Gifts).

CONSIDERATION: Catholic Action (Education, Literature, Social Work).

THIRD MEDITATION: The Incarnation (Man, God, Nazareth).

✠

THE VIRGIN'S SONG
TO HER BABY CHRIST.

(Adapted from Early English.)

Et Regina mater sua nichil habuit unde posset eum induere, ideo dixit sibi:

Jesu, sweet son ever dear,
On poor bed liest Thou there,
   And that me grieveth sore;
Thy cradle as a bier,
Ox and ass thy fere *(company)*,
   Weep must I therefore.

Jesu, sweet, be not wroth,
Though I have clout nor cloth,
   Thee wherein to fold,
To fold Thee, nor to wrap,
But huddle to my lap,
   And shield Thee from the cold.

———

FOURTH DAY, FIRST MEDITATION:

DEATH AND JUDGMENT.

IT may help us to imagine a Dead Mass proceeding, and beneath the pall and inside the coffin our own body. We are not sure even of a Dead Mass; we might, for example, lose our lives in a storm at sea. Still, it may help us to bring our death home to ourselves so to picture the matter. It is so difficult to move ourselves off the stage of life! One would think that we had received a private assurance that our services were indispensable! No, we must jam it into a coffin with conviction, this body of ours, these very limbs which now seem so much our own. The Requiem will also remind us of the graver and more solemn side of death, being not only a preliminary to the stowing away of our bodies, but a harbinger of their resurrection, and above all, the solemn prayer of the Church for the welfare of our soul. We beg for the grace to fashion our lives now, in thought and word and deed, as we shall wish to have fashioned them in death and at judgment. This is a meditation which especially confirms our purpose of amendment.

It may be noticed that little is said in the course of it about Purgatory, any more than in the course of the meditation on Hell. Within the short compass of our retreat it is not pos-

sible to touch upon every topic, but in the
course of the year fuller justice may be done
to all subjects, and none omitted. Even now
some may find the thought of that cleansing
fire a help and may desire to introduce it, and
the profit which they expect to derive from so
doing is a sufficient justification. The thought
of Purgatory may serve as a warning to us not
to make light even of small sins; or again it
may excite us to a lively sympathy with the
suffering souls, and to generous action towards
them. Indeed, in such a devotion as the *Heroic
Act* both ends may be secured, since the very
renunciation, so far as in us lies, of what may
lighten our Purgatory, will make us the more
careful not to increase it. 'This heroic act of
charity in behalf of the souls in Purgatory', to
quote the Raccolta (*Engl. Transl.*, 1915, p. 352),
'consists in a voluntary offering, made by any
one of the faithful in their favour, of all works
of satisfaction done by him in this life, as well
as of all suffrages which shall be offered for
him after his death; by this act he deposits
all these works and suffrages into the hands
of the Blessed Virgin, that she may distribute
them in behalf of those holy souls whom it is
her good pleasure to deliver from the pains of
Purgatory, at the same time that he declares
that by this personal offering he only foregoes
in their behalf the special and personal benefit

of these works of satisfaction, so that, if he is a priest, he is not hindered from applying the Holy Sacrifice of the Mass according to the intention of those who give him alms for that purpose.'

DEATH. Death is certain. If we could but persuade ourselves that our death was really coming, it would be almost enough to make saints of us by itself. It is coming, and coming quickly. How many landmarks have we not already passed, that at one time seemed so far off! Religious life has many such landmarks, steps in our career that have reference either to our spiritual progress, our studies, or holy orders. As surely as we have passed these by, one by one, so that they are now mere incidents in our past history, so surely it will come to be that, either through sickness or some accident, either suddenly or after previous ailment, our soul will leave our body, we shall be judged, it will be Heaven, Purgatory, or Hell. Perhaps that event is not so far off as the stage whence we first regarded wistfully our present position.

There are some thoughts, such as the above, which may help to bring home to us this certainty of death. There is a charm in round numbers; and we may, if we choose, pitch upon a round number, and ask ourselves, what about 2000 A.D.? It is a generous limit for our existence, and should carry conviction. What the world will have come to by that time, Heaven only knows; but we, at least, shall not be there. Few, if any, will know where are our mortal remains, and they will not be lovely to behold. And meanwhile, heedless of our bones, the world will still be going its way, doubtless business and politics and pleasure will still be thought the only things worth caring about, and we — what will it matter to us? Will it be well with us, well as it was never well before? Or shall we lie under another, an appalling doom?

Or again, look at the matter in another way. Must not many feel that they are hurrying to that dissolution, that their limbs no longer have the spring of youth, that much is now difficult which once was easy? We bear about with us the answer of death. It need not be a funeral march that our hearts beat, but it is certainly a march to the grave. Nor are we singular in this. Many, at least, have passed their prime, and death is tightening its grip upon them. We need not think that every little ailment is to be our last, but it would be foolish to ignore the lesson altogether, and not to consider whither all these little troubles point.

One more thought. It may help us to realise our own death if we reflect on the great world, or worlds, of souls that lie beyond. For of all the millions of men that have walked this earth since Adam, none have wholly ceased to be. The Jews of the Old Testament, the Greeks and Romans of classical times, the Franks, our own forefathers; the patriarchs and prophets, all the saints of the new Covenant, all the great warriors and statesmen of whom we have read; all these, and all mankind, have stood in their turn before the Divine Judge, and have been requited according to their works. They live no less than we, though no longer in the flesh. And we shall join this vast host. Only there is a yawning gulf that cleaves it, and he that would pass over may not do so. Cyrus, Alexander, Caesar, they live — but on which side of that chasm? And so we might pass through history, remembering that it is living beings of whom we read. How poignant the thought can become, whether in the case of a character that has enthralled us, or of those we knew! But we too shall pass over yonder; and which of those arrays is it to be? Oh that we might say with the poor and humble Francis, 'The saints are waiting for me, till Thou call me.'

But there is the uncertainty of death too. It may be useful to think out a few possible deaths, widely different from each other in all their circumstances, even in the time of life at which they befall us. This may help to bring home to us the extent of our ignorance. And not merely is the manner of our death unknown to us now, but death is only too likely to be unexpected when it actually comes. Christ Himself urges this truth upon us. And is it not a matter of experience, that even they who die after a long illness do not realise that the end is upon them? It is in the nature of man to cling so hard to life that even without any fault of his own he fails to realise the true state of affairs. 'Thou fool! This night they ask thy life of thee!' (Luke XII, 20). It is not only the wicked who may show themselves foolish in this respect; the good sometimes fail to bring it home to themselves that their eternity is not to be in this world. In the first place, one must not underestimate the risk; it has never been very difficult to lose one's life in this world. In the second place, we cannot over-estimate the importance of the catastrophe when it does come. Sober fact is more than enough for us. But to appreciate better the significance of death, we must now turn our thoughts to what follows it, namely, Christ's judgment upon our soul.

THE PARTICULAR JUDGMENT. And first to form an accurate idea of what that judgment is. The Fathers of the Church and the preachers of all ages often speak as though it were a long business, the devil and our angel guardian appearing as witnesses, and so forth. This is a vivid way of presenting to the Christian people truths which it is hard to push home in any other form.

Christ, the Word, the everlasting Wisdom of the
Father, has been given all judgment as man,
inasmuch as in His human nature He is Redeemer
and King of mankind, and the Head of the
Church.   But it is not to be supposed that
whenever a human soul leaves the body, He at
once betakes Himself thither, ever flitting from
dead to dead.   Much less can it be conceived
that the soul appears before Him in heaven;
that were the beatific vision.   It is enough that
the soul should be made clearly aware of its
own merits and demerits, of the fact that Christ
has passed sentence upon it.   It appears before
Him intellectually, not locally; in a moment the
whole of its past life stands clear before it, and
in the same moment it is made aware of the
verdict as coming from Him.   The hubbub of
the world is hushed, its false principles find no
advocate, the passions burn no more. lies have
no place, now is the triumph of truth.   The
conscience is open, every thought, word and deed
as it was in actual fact, and it is clear as noonday
what the just sentence must be.   We shall stand
before Christ, in a new relation to Him, but in
one that is the complement of our present relation.
This is the time of mercy, but it is mercy in
view of that judgment; that judgment is ever
drawing nearer, and we are ever writing our
condemnation or acquittal. And Christ will enforce
justice; we can imagine Him without smile or

welcome, simply intent upon His duty, like a friend in retreat. No frailty escapes Him. Every offence will be punished, that is to say, it is not passed over unless there has been adequate contrition and satisfaction, with confession in so far as it was necessary and possible. On the other hand He never goes beyond our guilt; there are no rash conclusions to be feared, as there might be in the case of a mere man.

If, then, this judgment is to be decided aright, it is clear what must be done. We must adopt now the standard according to which we shall then be judged. In this lies the chief fruit of this meditation. Death and judgment will clear up our ideas as nothing yet, and the mere thought of them is illuminating. It teaches us the wickedness and folly of sin. How shall we picture to ourselves the distraction of a soul that finds itself before its Judge with the deep stain of mortal sin! And what shall we think of venial sin? What can come of it save shame and confusion, the confession of our senseless neglect, regret for so many graces lost for ever? Even in our best actions, how much we shall find of self and of less worthy motives, so little indifference to creatures, so little whole-hearted striving after our one end, the greater glory of God!

THE LAST JUDGMENT. We may conclude with some thoughts upon the Last Judgment. Is is to be preceded by several signs, of which one may read in the New Testament; and more immediately by the resurrection of the body. The peculiar significance of the Last Judgment may be said to lie in this, that man will be judged before his fellow-creatures, and in relation to them. The fruit of every good and bad action will be seen, carried down perhaps through centuries. We cannot rid ourselves of responsibility for others; we are perpetually influencing all about us, even in a religious community, for good or for evil, either we are helping or hindering the work of personal sanctification. It is then that we shall understand the value of good example, the value of religious education, of apostolic suffering and prayer. The founders of the great religious families will also receive a full measure of honour from the thousands of their children, who have learnt from them the way of perfection. And on the other hand the vengeance with which Our Lord has threatened him who should scandalise his brother, that is, cause him to sin, will also be beheld. The full mischief of the scarcely perceptible sneer will be plain, and much more the havoc wrought by deliberate temptation and perversion, whether for the sake of pleasure or gain — what shall we say of those who have wrenched whole peoples away from the Church, or plucked the faith from the hearts of children? There will be a mountain of sin at their door, unless they can plead good faith or repentance.

8 *

Does the good that we have worked among our fellow-men exceed the evil? Every man is the apostle of his own principles, of the principles, that is, which really govern his conduct. The more sacred and responsible our position, the more we must fear the effect of our shortcomings.

God will triumph, in that the very nature of sin and virtue will be evident beyond excuse or jest or cavil — the true inwardness of anger, covetousness, sensuality, and again of suffering and shame borne for His sake. We pray to understand these things here and now; that is our petition as we turn to our crucifix, which alone can teach us how it is that we have been spared so far, and still have time to learn.

FOURTH DAY, SECOND MEDITATION:

CHRIST THE KING.

Abstract ideals do not easily move us. We are creatures of flesh and blood, and need to have our ideals clothed in flesh and blood, or at least in concrete personality. And our Heavenly Father, who knows so well every inarticulate yearning of our nature, has met this need. He met it even under the old Covenant. The more undeveloped a people, the more they need to have even the natural law presented to them as direct revelation. And to the Jews God was ever manifesting Himself as a Person acting in their midst, as one who loved righteousness and hated iniquity, who loved them and watched over them, their Shepherd, their King. The theocracy, the immediate government of God, meant personal contact with Him. That contact, however, was not close enough for His love, nor, if we may put it thus, was virtue and holiness impersonated to the full extent which divine wisdom and mercy could devise. It was something to conceive of the good as being loved by the Lord God with an active and boundless love; it was far more that God should come down to earth and display true goodness to us, not only as His all-holy pleasure, but in Himself, the goodness of God manifesting itself in human thoughts and deeds. So the Word became Flesh.

THE NEW FOUNDATION. In these exercises we have not, it is true, been wholly abstracting from the Incarnation. That had been too stern. On the contrary, cut to the heart with shame and remorse for our own sinfulness, we found in the Crucified our only solace and our only hope, and to Him we poured out all that the sight of His pain and of His love prompted in us. The main body of our meditation, on the other hand, had not yet any very marked reference to Him. He rather appeared at the end to save us from being overwhelmed by the crushing weight of thoughts which at first had to be considered apart from Himself, that we might see them in their naked truth, their awful reality. And even as the gleam of hope, ever softening the dreadful punishments under the First Law, burst forth upon the shepherds in the glory of the God made man, so now that saving thought of redemption is to fill the whole canvas, we are to lose ourselves in the love of Christ, itself the supreme love of God, and able to strengthen and establish all lesser feelings which should go with it. This is the new foundation which we are now about to lay. We must not let go our hold upon those first principles which are the foundation of the whole of the retreat, and which are deduced from a clear conception of the end of man. These and the like will only be emphasized and enforced in the following of Christ and under His teaching. But our chief concern is to greet our new King and swear Him our homage, to confess how far we have fallen from what we now see to be our true ideal, to thank Him that He did not leave us in our desperate plight, but had pity on us, put Himself at the head of the broken battalions of the human race, and is now ready to lead us to sure victory. We can regain all that we had lost, and conquer fresh domains.

THE CALL. Saint Ignatius, the soldier-saint of Pampeluna, his very holiness and love of Christ instinct with all the martial ardour of Spanish chivalry, does indeed present us these thoughts under the parable of a holy war, proclaimed by a God-given captain. The idea was a fairly familiar one in his time. The head of the Holy Roman Empire was, nominally at least, the temporal head of the whole of Christendom. The crusades were also still present to the minds of all, the more so because the danger from the Turk was still serious; and the memory of such a general as Saint Louis of France cannot have been wholly dead. Moreover there were closer parallels of present date, the rumours of which must have filled the air, the conquests of Cortes in Mexico and Pizarro in Peru, not to speak of Columbus himself. And all the cruelty and avarice that marred the work of colonisation and the spread of the Gospel could only be a reminder that in following Christ we must have but a single interest and purpose.

At the very outset we are shown what is the true call to which we have to lend ear, and of which any temporal call can be but a figure. For it is no earthly mustering-place that we picture to ourselves, but the scene of Our Lord's own labours, synagogue and town and village in the Holy Land, symbolic of vaster labours throughout all time and space. And we pray to hear His call, to be ready and eager to carry out His most holy Will.

First, then, this temporal leader, human, yet with a divine sanction and a heavenly purpose. All men owe him obedience; yet he does not compel them, but calls for volunteers. He wishes to subdue all the territory of the infidels, from upright and holy motives, that they may all receive spiritual care and become members of the true Church. Such a purpose was well understood in the days of Saint Ignatius; yet then, as now, it was too often rather in spite of their conquerors that savages were converted to Christianity. But here there can be no misconception. Victory and success are sure. Only one thing is asked, that they who follow the chief should be content to have the same food and clothing as he, to work and watch as he — but not more than he. No very stringent condition! To such a generous appeal all but cowards eagerly respond. How inspiring is the rush of a nation to arms! We appear to be returning to the old idea, that every citizen should be ready to do battle for his country at need. But even the call of patriotism is spiritless compared to the call of a crusade such as we here imagine, when all the deepest religious emotions are also profoundly stirred. '*Dieu le veut!*' It is the call of God!

Jesus Christ is our Lord and our eternal King; before Him is the whole world, and to each and all He makes His appeal. He wishes to have it for Himself, to subdue it all, and so to enter into His Father's glory. Physically, so to speak, His sovereignty over the world is already absolute, but it is a spiritual conquest that He desires, the winning of man through man's free choice. It is an enterprise of love, love for those whom He would subdue, love for those who offer themselves as His comrades — indeed, in these latter He would also establish His kingdom more firmly. It is an enterprise of suffering — suffering there must be, but it is suffering with Christ, and a suffering that surely leads to glory, also with Him. Long ago He began to enlist His followers, and who shall tell all the love and devotion with which He has met? And those who gave it were right. It is right and reasonable to be a Christian, to proclaim ourselves followers of Christ, to know, to love, to serve Him; and they are most right and most reasonable who give Him the most of their best. It cannot but profit and ennoble them; to renounce all for Christ is to find all again in Him.

GREATER GIFTS. There are, then, those who endeavour to serve their Lord with greater generosity. They may not feel that they have very much to give, but at least they are determined to keep nothing back. They have found a cause to which to devote themselves, a leader in whom they believe with their whole heart, for whom they are ready to live and to die. They will not be content with mediocrity. Mediocrity, in so far as it means something less than our best, is a thing always despicable. No man need resign himself to it, for all can 'make their lives sublime'. It argues either an object not worth striving after, or a lack of perception in him who is striving after it. The Christian always has something worth living for, and that something is Christ.

To Christ, then, we desire to cling with utter devotion, and to offer Him the best service that we can; and the question at once arises, how? The soldier may be eager to get at the enemy, forgetful of self; but ours is a peculiar warfare, and there is a sense in which we cannot afford to lose sight of our own selves. After all, even a soldier's first duty is to be ready at the call of obedience; he must not take it for granted that he is always to join in the actual fighting. And again, the more important the work for which he is destined, the longer and severer must be his training. We, on our side, may be said to have a fight always awaiting us; but only if it be first understood that we are our own truceless foe. We may wish to embark upon some spiritual enterprise that will make a show in the world; but we cannot grasp too firmly that vital truth, that it is not what we do that matters, but what we are. And it will need prolonged and patient effort to make of ourselves soldiers after our Leader's own heart. It is in our own souls that we must establish Christ's Kingdom ever more firmly. When He is truly Lord there, the battle will have been won; for He is certain to secure anything that

He wishes from those who are wholly His. In this sense all our zeal for Christ must be directed upon our own selves. *Attende tibi!*

On the other hand it must be understood that this zeal for oneself is not exclusive, but rather inclusive, nay, all-embracing. In this sense it is truly apostolic, but apostolic on the right lines, full of love for Christ and neighbour, but for the neighbour by reason of Christ; looking therefore first to Christ for guidance, and not rushing into action without heed of the word of command. It is a zeal strong and strenuous, yet under strong and strenuous control, ready to take what part in the great warfare may be given it, without craving immoderately for immediate or very tangible results. It can be seen in a Teresa no less than in a Xavier. Speaking generally, indeed, even in apostolic work it is the quality more than the quantity of the results that matters; the perfection of the few is a greater work, albeit often less showy, than the slighter improvement of the many, because any person that is truly holy will bear ample fruit of his own. But from zeal and keenness itself nothing can excuse; there is no place in the service of Christ for languor or cynicism, whether in general behaviour or conversation. There is always so much to be keen about, and to be bored is as unworthy as it is miserable. There must be no false humility, such as his who deprecates religious observance as fit only for saints, and not for the likes of him, or who will not try a difficult work, but only something below his capacity, something in which he is practically sure of success. Nor, on the other hand, may there be a reckless desire for publicity, any more than for pleasure in any other shape. Always, in a word, our service must be to Christ our King, and for His sake we must be prepared for all and refuse nothing, so only that we can spread His Kingdom; and to do this we need, as has been said, to attend first and foremost, and all the time, to ourselves, though not in such a manner as really to exclude work upon others.

And once more we ask, how? How are we to perfect Christ's Kingdom within us? His is a kingdom of love, and love is ever seeking to express itself through suffering. What are we ready to bear for Christ? It is a warfare that we undertake for Him, a warfare with Him for leader. Our enemies are very real, the Devil, the World, and the Flesh; there can be no doubt that it is a warfare in which brave suffering will be necessary if we are to win. Here then we have the offering which we are to make to Christ. It is an offering which we shall have to understand better, to make more generously, as we proceed; for we are to penetrate ourselves more and more with Christ's own spirit, to watch Him and learn from Him, to love Him and unite ourselves with Him. But already we make the substantial offering of ourselves, and therewith lay this fresh foundation, which is to serve for the rest of the retreat. It is a solemn offering, made before Almighty God aud our Blessed Mother Mary and all the heavenly court. It is an offering to follow our Divine Leader, to follow whither He has led, to battle as He has battled, to suffer as He has suffered. It is a protestation that for Him and with Him we are ready for all hardships and reproaches and injuries. Our only care is to be His, and to follow His least wish.

FOURTH DAY, CONSIDERATION:
CATHOLIC ACTION.

At this stage in our retreat, when we have just been considering Christ's summons, and are about to see in Him what it truly means, it is well for us to turn our thoughts for a while to a subject which has no very direct bearing upon our own sanctification, but which it is very important that we should understand aright, namely, Catholic action, Catholic public action, that united effort which Catholics ought to make, in order to play their part in the public life of the nation. If they are to do this, it is vital that there should be a healthy public opinion on the subject among themselves, and religious can do much to give a right lead in the matter. It is much to be lamented, that religious themselves, for one reason or another, sometimes show but little concern for what are, in reality, the vital interests of Christ and His Church.

Catholic action may take many forms, but we may content ourselves with three departments that are very important in themselves, and under which Catholic action of every kind could perhaps be brought, namely, education, literature and social work. But first, by way of preface, it may be well to say a few words on the need of unity. The unity which Christ asked for His Church was a unity comparable only to the unity between Himself and the Father (John XVII, 21—23), a unity therefore by no means exhausted by the essential organisation and teaching of the Church, but an ideal to be kept before one in all else besides. The children of darkness, Our Lord tells us (Luke XVI, 8), are wiser in their generation than the children of light; and nothing is more lamentable than to see how all the enemies of the Church at once combine when there is question of an attack upon her, while even when the attack penetrates to all that should be nearest and dearest to them, Catholics sometimes remain miserably and unworthily divided, and so fail to offer that capable resistance which one would expect from their numbers and influence. It is owing to this that the interests of Christ and His Church have suffered so grievously in France and elsewhere, and not least in our own country. If any one who stirs up war between class and class is working for the Devil, there must be some deeper hell reserved for those who incite one class of Catholics against another, even if they be lay folk, and much more if they be consecrated to God's service. Religious, then, must be zealous for Catholic peace and unity, and even be prepared to make great sacrifices for it; and they should endeavour to infect all others with a like spirit. Much can be done by mutual sympathy; and if ever two parties both think it right in Our Lord to press opposing claims, they should still remember that it is a mark and privilege of the Church to preserve external unity, and that there is always an authority to whom disputes ought to be referred for final settlement. But to carry on anything like an agitation inside the Church against other members of it is to serve the Devil.

EDUCATION. It is of the last importance that Catholics, and most of all religious, should form to themselves a true ideal of education. It is of course right that a certain amount of knowledge should be imparted to children; but that is not the most important function of education, and it would be a monstrous abuse were the general welfare of body and soul to suffer for the sake

of it. As a matter of fact the better sort of
education aims less at instilling information than
at training the faculties, so that the work of
after-life may be done well and intelligently. In
the intellectual sphere nothing can make up for
a defective instrument, and our object should
be rather a mind that will work well upon what
may be presented to it than a mind overladen
with barren facts. And this truth has a far
more urgent application in the moral sphere,
or rather — for to speak of the 'moral sphere' is
unduly to narrow the issue — in the whole life
of the whole man. It is not what a man knows
or does not know, can do or cannot do, that
really matters, but what he is, his character,
and his whole outlook upon eternity. And hence
it is that there are few things more radically
immoral than the demand that there should be
no tests for teachers. Indeed, taken as it stands,
the demand is so preposterous that few if any
would venture to associate themselves with it.
The man who should din into men's ears that
it was a horrible injustice to demand that any
one who was to teach mathematics should know
something about it, would be thought fit for an
asylum; and yet this is what is going on in regard of things immeasurably more important than
mathematics. It is the religious principles of a
man that matter more than all else; the experience of the ages shows that nothing else

can brace up his soul to high thoughts or resolves. And unless a definite religion be taught
in the schools, the nation will be plunged into
a cynical materialism that can only lead to im-
patient persecution of all that is noblest in life.
We need not look very far abroad to see how
the process works. Many panaceas are constantly
being suggested for modern evils; but the long
and short of it is, that the character of a nation
depends largely upon the character of its schools,
and where the former are without God the whole
people will know nothing of Him.

But care must be taken that the Catholic
religion is really taught in Catholic schools,
whether primary or secondary; taught by example
and the whole environment, and also by definite
and carefully planned instruction, so that the
children know their faith well, and know the
answers to the commonest difficulties against it.
A child that has not been taught its religion
properly is helpless before a chance companion
or halfpenny press; to safeguard it, not merely
doctrine is needed, but a certain amount of Holy
Scripture and Church History too. There is a
great danger that examinations may crowd out
what most needs to be taught. The primary
use of Catholic schools is to turn out fervent
and well-grounded Catholics.

LITERATURE. Catholic literature may be looked
at from two points of view, that of the writers

and that of the readers. As regards writers, we have not a few of note among those that have passed away, and it should be a point of honour with Catholics not to suffer their memory to fade; but it is also vital that there should be sufficient writers in every age to present the Catholic point of view with force and precision. Work of this indirect kind is only too likely to be underrated, as compared with work which brings in more immediate and tangible results. It should be remembered that for one person reached in personal intercourse or preaching, a hundred may often be reached by writing, though the writing also needs to be well circulated. Writers may conveniently be classified under two main heads, experts, who write about subjects which they have made their serious study, and those whom we may without depreciation call journalistic writers, who write about subjects which they have 'got up', or about their own experiences or other matters which do not call for prolonged preparation. Religious can do a great work in both these departments; there are magazines of many kinds that may usefully be kept going, and indeed the question might be raised whether nuns might not do rather more in this, as in some other kinds of writing. But whenever religious write, they should make it their care, when there is a favourable opening, to present the Catholic standpoint in an accurate and pleasing way.

Now, on the whole, there is little fault to be
found with the supply of Catholic literature;
considering our numbers, it is surprisingly good,
though indeed it could hardly attain its present
level were there not also a market for Catholic
works in the United States and elsewhere. But
the demand needs to be doubled and trebled,
and opportunity should be taken, both at school
and afterwards, to impress upon Catholics their
duty and their need in this respect. It is sad
to see so many abandoning themselves to useless and frivolous literature, when there is so
much that they might read with immense profit
to themselves and their neighbours. Nor can it
be said that this more profitable literature is
inaccessible or indigestible; the Catholic Truth
Society, for example, is doing a magnificent
work, which of itself refutes the charge. We
need not ask Catholics to give up papers and
periodicals; but it is not right to immerse oneself in those which are constantly presenting
views in one way or another anti-Catholic, and
to neglect those which consistently present and
defend the Catholic point of view. Such a proceeding may very easily lead to the Catholic
point of view being lost sight of altogether.
And there is plenty of Catholic fiction which is
positively helpful — works by 'John Ayscough',
Mgr. Benson, Canon Sheehan, and a host of
others. Religious should train those under their

9 *

charge to a taste for Catholic writings (why
should not prizes at school be confined to such?)
and encourage all others in the same direction.

SOCIAL WORK. Evidently one can do little more
than allude to this great subject; and perhaps
that is as much as is needed in a retreat. The
publications of the Catholic Social Guild will give
valuable guidance to those who seek it, and the
chief function of a retreat in this matter is to
awaken one to the gravity of the issues involved.
If Christianity is to be applied to the life of the
people, if the Church is still to be a living
force, not merely must the Gospel itself be
preached, but the practical application of its
precepts to the lives of the people must also
be insisted on. It is not the function of the
Church to keep the masses quiet, while the classes
proceed to enjoy themselves; it is her province
to explain to all their rights as well as their
duties, and to encourage them to attain them,
at all events when they are so bound up with
morality as in the case of the living wage, and
other such questions vital for the Christian family. No doubt this means that more money
must pass from rich to poor, and the former
may be alarmed accordingly; but in the long
run interests are identical, for permanent peace
can only be found when the mass of the people
have a sufficient and secure wage. Nor, when
we speak of the working classes, must we con-

fine our attention to the plutocracy of labour, to workmen protected by strong trade unions, which are only too liable to abuse their power. The true evil is to be found in the condition of those too badly paid to be able to organise themselves. It is the business of the Church, not merely to aid the weak and poor, but to defend them.

FOURTH DAY, THIRD MEDITATION:
THE INCARNATION.

We now come to consider the Incarnation more at large, to ponder how and why our Saviour took flesh. The meditation has three aspects. It is natural, in the first place, to reflect upon man, and the desperate straits to which he had brought himself. Then we contemplate the divine action in the matter. God did not leave man in his sorry plight, but determined to give him fresh and ample opportunities of extricating himself. And after that we have Nazareth, the link binding earth to heaven. It is there that the Word is made flesh in the womb of the Virgin-Mother, that God offers the supreme remedy for the ills and offences of a ruined world. Such is the threefold picture that we have before us in this meditation. We endeavour to penetrate the full significance of its several parts in turn, and to find food for reflection in each. Here, as in most other contemplations (that is, where something is being enacted which we can watch), we may pass over in our mind the persons, words and actions that come into consideration. We thus put out feelers, as it were, to see what there is to lay hold of. There is no need to divide the whole contemplation into watertight compartments; we may follow the trend of our thoughts without much scruple as to arrangement, provided they do not take us on to matters utterly foreign to the matter in hand. In the present case it may be more convenient, as it is simpler, to work each aspect out by itself.

MAN. St. Paul, writing to the Roman Church upon the new life of grace offered to all mankind through the Incarnation, opens with a terrible denunciation of the world as he knew it. The vices of the pagans, and especially their impurity, he attributes to their idolatry as the ultimate cause. They might have come to know God; His invisible attributes are to be contemplated in the visible world. And because they shut their eyes to Him, God in turn forsook them; He would not encompass them with that ample grace which would have brought them through all dangers, but merely gave them enough, and little more. They were free; they might have resisted temptation, they understood enough to incur serious guilt. But victory was no longer sweet and easy; they had forfeited the privilege of easy conquest, and with it they lost in large measure the victory itself.

And the Jews were little better. St. Paul will not suffer them to sit in judgment upon the sins of the gentiles, like the pharisee upon the publican. Speaking of his own nation in the lump, as he had spoken of the gentiles in the lump, he lays it down that they too are in sin, and themselves commit some of the serious offences for which they condemn the gentiles. But he especially condemns their notion of justification, the idea that external works, and more particularly among the Jews themselves the works of the Mosaic Law, can give any one a claim against God. He sets it forth that what is necessary first and before all is union with Christ.

As for the Jews, we know much about them from Holy Writ, both as regards the time of Our Lord and earlier. The gentiles referred to by St. Paul are primarily those of his own hellenistic world, the Greek-speaking population of Palestine, Syria, Asia Minor, the Aegaean, and Greece itself. Yet he doubtless meant his remarks to have a wider scope, and to some extent we may apply them to all paganism before the coming of Christ. Speaking very broadly, we may say that there was anarchy alike in thought and conduct. Religion had become hopelessly depraved, teaching for the most part many gods, and teaching all manner of unworthy

things about them; failing to teach mankind a
sound morality, largely because there were puri-
fications and consecrations which were supposed
to guard against the consequences of evil, but
in no way implied its renunciation. Philosophy
where it prevailed realised in part the grossness
of these abuses, and stood aloof from religion,
but, as always, remained ineffective without it,
unable to sustain prolonged sacrifice in more than
a few individuals, or to exercise any appreciable
influence upon the masses. And so morality was
at a low ebb; many of the vices varied according
to time and place, but almost everywhere that
one was dominant to which St. Paul most emphati-
cally points, impurity.

Such as was the world before Christ, such also
it is today without Him. The more Christianity
is cast forth, under the guise of impartial unde-
nominationalism, the more the beast in man breaks
out, and not least in this very matter of impurity;
it is not difficult to adapt the words of the Apostle
to our own time. Nor to ourselves also; for
without Christ we are full of sin, and of the
promise of sin. We can measure our need of
Him by our actual dependence upon Him, and
all we feel that He has brought us, and even
by the faults and follies that yet remain. To
understand better our own need, as also that of
the world, whether in the time of Christ or in
our own, we may find it a help to build upon

former meditations, the neglect of the fundamental principles we first considered, the guilt of sin committed, the horror of the punishment incurred.

GOD. Having this general idea of the sunken state of man, a state which we can gauge to some small extent by the neo-paganism of our own time, we may now turn to consider what view God took of the matter. Of one thing we can be absolutely certain, that all this vast and accumulating heap of sin was utterly abominable in His eyes. If we take the most Christian times, the catalogue of the world's yearly, nay, daily crimes must have been a terrible one; what then shall we say, for instance, of the great Roman empire, at the time when monsters like Gaius or Nero were absolute rulers setting the tone of the capital, when slavery robbed a very large proportion of mankind of any right save that to do their master's pleasure, when so many other evils were rampant?

And yet God, for all His infinite holiness, turned to mercy. He need not have done so. He might have exacted the last farthing of the debt, and have condemned to eternal torment all who had incurred grievous guilt, without providing any special help to diminish the number of those condemned. The largeness of the number could never affect either His infinite perfection or His infinite happiness. Or again, God might have freely pardoned all the past, and forthwith have provided a far ampler store of graces for the future. We cannot and dare not circumscribe God's freedom, any more than His justice or His mercy. But in the way He actually took there was a marvellous blending of all these. The outrage committed against the Divine Majesty was in a manner infinite, the distance between Him and His creatures being itself in a manner infinite. And so the reparation itself was to be in a manner infinite; the offending creature was to offer a sufficient reparation, by itself being identified with the infinite majesty of the Creator. The reparation offered by the God-man was thus to be sufficient for all, and the Divine Mercy was to have free play toward those who would avail themselves of this vicarious satisfaction, who, in the language of the Apostle, would become one with Christ upon His Cross, crucifying their old self, that with Christ they might rise in a new and divine life. And so the Word became flesh, the second Person of the Blessed Trinity became man; yet not only to offer that supreme act of atonement, but also to teach us by His example and precept how to order our own lives, and to leave behind Him in the Church ever-flowing fountains of grace, chief among them the sacred banquet of His own Body and Blood, and also many other means of sanctification and salvation.

Once again let us turn the matter to our own case. And how can we think without a shudder of a life unpitied by God, with a fair chance but nothing more? 'We all do cry for mercy.' Let not our attitude be that of the Pharisee, reckoning up our good works against God rather than seeking them at His hand. Let us confess how much we owe to His grace, to His mercy upon the human race and upon ourselves, in order that so benign a flood may flow more freely still.

NAZARETH. If we consider the vast issues of which we have been speaking, mankind sunk in misery, in sin, and God resolved to redeem, we might expect gigantic preparations to be set on foot for the execution of the divine plan. And such indeed there were. The conquests of Alexander had made Greek the common language of the East, and when Rome united the civilised world under her imperial sway, she did not endeavour to oust the hellenistic civilisation and language, but rather herself learnt it. With this community of language and thought, and with the Jewish dispersion spread far and wide, the way was paved for the rapid spread of the Gospel. Nor was this all the *praeparatio evangelica*: Divine Providence prepared the world for Christ in many other ways. And yet it would have appeared preposterous to Greek or Roman that a great deliverer should have his birth in despised Judaea.

For our part, looking upon the Old Testament
with the eye of faith, we could not imagine
anything else; yet even we should not have
looked to Nazareth. We cannot but surmise that
its reputation did not stand high (John I, 46);
this may have been due in part to the traffic
that passed through along the 'Way of the
Sea', doubtless bringing with it many bent on
commerce and money-making, pagan and Jew.
Yet Nazareth stood in the midst of a country
beautiful in itself, and hallowed by many Old
Testament memories, and was itself a priest-centre,
in close touch therefore with the Temple at Jerusalem.

'Hail, full of grace!' It was a mighty arch-
angel, worthy, if a creature could be, to bear
that supreme message of Divine purpose. It was
a young woman of no great wealth or power
or accomplishments that received it; yet at her
very conception she had been prepared for this
moment, and that rich store of grace which the
angel signified must have singled her out for the
observant. And now she has but one anxiety,
her virginity, until she is told the mystery that
is to be wrought in her. And then, overwhelmed,
she has but one word, of deep humility and
obedience: 'Behold the handmaid of the Lord,
be it done to me according to thy word.' That
was enough; even thus it befell, and the angel
left her.

We may address such prayers as it occurs to us to make, to the most Holy Trinity, to the Mother of God, to the Word made flesh. We may pray more especially that the Divine purpose of the Incarnation may be accomplished in our regard to the uttermost.

FIFTH DAY.

THE GOSPEL.

PATRON: Our Blessed Lady.

READING: Mark I; I Cor. XII-XIII; Imitation III, 54-55.

FIRST MEDITATION: The Nativity (The Baptist, The Birth, The Guests).

SECOND MEDITATION: The Two Standards (Satan, Christ).

CONSIDERATION: The Triple Cord (Gentleman, Scholar, Saint).

THIRD MEDITATION: The Holy Family (The World, Family Life, God).

✠

THE MONTH OF MAY.

In the month of May
Life stirs in every seed
That from earth's womb
Seeks still to rise and bloom,
From coffined darkness to be freed.

In the month of May,
The bud, burst all too soon,
Bows a frail form
To bear the nightlong storm
And live unto a summer noon.

Be thou our May,
Pierce through the cloying sod,
Through chilly night
Lead us to hallowed light,
To the dear bosom of our God.

FIFTH DAY, FIRST MEDITATION:

THE NATIVITY.

UNDER this heading we may continue the narrative from the time of the Incarnation. The central event is the birth of Christ; we consider some of the intermediate events, and the visit of the shepherds, which immediately followed it. The scene is a shifting one — the home of Elizabeth, Nazareth, the way to Bethlehem, Bethlehem itself, the stable, shepherds in the fields, the Wise Men that speed along the desert way. We make the contemplation in the spirit of the meditation on Christ the King. He is our Divine Leader, about to enter upon the war. We pray that we make His plan of campaign our own, follow out His methods, execute His wishes, reckon naught of sacrifices in His cause. In a word, we pray that we may know Him more clearly, love Him more dearly, follow Him more nearly.

THE BAPTIST. Before the annunciation to Mary there had been an annunciation to Zachary. Mary herself heard directly from the angel that she was to conceive without loss of virginity; but the birth of the Baptist was fitly announced to Zachary as to the head of the family, though the child-bearing of Elizabeth was itself to some extent contrary to nature. Mary was at some ordinary avocation, perhaps at prayer; Zachary

LATTEY, Thy Love. 10

was burning incense in the Holy Place, for the
first and last time. It was the supreme moment
in an ordinary priest's life, for there were too
many of them for any to be allowed to perform
the function twice. Mary was bewildered, knowing well that an All-Holy God would never
have her renounce her virginity; none the less she
believed, and in this regard Elizabeth had good
cause to call her blessed, for Zachary lay under
punishment for doubt. Yet Zachary's was no
mean privilege either, and we can understand
from the canticle that broke his silence how
perfectly he had borne his chastisement, and
how deep was his promised joy.

And now Mary comes to visit the aged pair;
for love brooks no delays, and Infinite Love abides
within her womb. Apparently Elizabeth knew
by revelation all that had befallen her kinswoman,
for when the infant in her womb leaped for joy,
she knew well what it portended. What we have
to admire in her, as in her son later, is the
mingled love and humility with which she greets
one greater before God than herself. And just
as Our Lord could never disclaim what the Baptist
said of Him, so Mary will not deny her unspeakable privilege. Yet she confesses in a beautiful
outpouring of thankfulness and humility that it
is to God that she owes all. Thus there is
everywhere humility: Zachary displays it under
his chastisement, Elizabeth humbles herself before

Mary, and Mary refers all to God. But Mary had also humbled herself in making the visit at all, involving as it doubtless did a not very easy journey, especially as there was little or no preparation for it; and she stayed to assist at the Baptist's birth. That, too, was to be remarkable, as was but fitting, seeing that he was the last prophet sent to Israel, and greater than all before. His was to be an austere life, his mission one great rebuke of sin and call to repentance; yet he was overflowing with tenderness for the 'Lamb of God'. But to his ministry we shall return anon.

THE BIRTH. Of her own accord Mary had faced the journey to Elizabeth and had rendered service; but when she returned she had to face a trial that might seem almost wanton cruelty, if Divine Providence could be guilty of this. St. Joseph had no knowledge of the mystery that had been wrought in her; he only perceived that she was with child. Thus, so shortly after this signal grace, which was to extend in such large measure to St. Joseph himself, God plunged both him and his betrothed into anguish, and forthwith required them to enter upon the royal road of the Cross. Their affliction was in proportion to their privilege. Affliction, therefore, need not be a sign of God's anger, but is the inevitable accompaniment of His love. And the same God that bestows it can amply repair it. St. Joseph needed guidance, for he was torn between his

10*

duty according to the Mosaic Law and his invincible belief in the virtue of his wife. After he had suffered awhile, he received the necessary instruction, and his soul was flooded with consolation, because Mary had found favour in God's sight beyond all that he could dream of. She became his wife, and their joy was full.

Then came fresh trouble. The birth of Christ was to be marked by poverty and persecution. It was probably the year 8 B. C., when the second great census of the Empire was being taken, and St. Joseph and Our Lady suddenly found themselves compelled to undertake a journey of eighty miles and more, in order that St. Joseph might register himself and his family. After a journey that St. Joseph must have found trying, and Our Lady still more so, they meet with a fresh disappointment. The caravansary at Bethlehem was full, full of those who could boast themselves to be of the house of David. They too had been brought thither by the census, and we need not suppose any fault on the part of those who turned the weary couple away. Still, another place had to be found, where the Divine Infant might be born; and it was found in a manger, which according to tradition belonged to a stable arranged in a cave. He is born, therefore, in utter destitution, He Who might have chosen the palaces of the Caesars or of the high-priests at Jerusalem. He has not come for

His own sake, but for ours; for our sake it is better that He should be the occasion of anguish to His parents, and Himself lack a human dwelling-place. From the manger He points to Calvary: He is to teach us to value suffering, suffering with and in Him. The manger is the chair whence He teaches the world, and as we kneel there we may tell Him how novel and how difficult is the lesson, and beg for all help in learning it.

THE GUESTS. In the shepherds Christ shows us what manner of pupils he desires. No procession wound its way out of Jerusalem, to greet Him with dance and melody. Yet He took the best of what the old order had to offer Him. The shepherds were the true representatives of the Old Testament. They led a pastoral life of simple faith. Doubtless they repaired to Jerusalem at the fixed times, and with overflowing heart sang praise and thanksgiving unto God amid the glories of His temple. They may well have known something of the abuses rife among the pharisees and the high-priestly families; they were grieved, but none the less showed priest and rabbi the deference due to them. In their ears rang the warnings and invitations of the prophets, and on their lips were the sacred psalms. Theirs was a simple and righteous life; Jehovah had their faith and their love, and blessed them for it. They were not the saints of the Old Covenant,

like Simeon and Anna, who were to find the
Lord in His holy temple, or the Baptist, who
was to proclaim Him in the wilderness. Rather
they represented the people as such, and all
that their religion could do for them; we may
think of the Catholic peasantry in many a province of Europe, whose simple farm pursuits
are blended with an inward, and even outward,
life that is deeply spiritual.

These were the men of God's good pleasure,
to whom an angel announced great joy, and
a multitude of his fellows peace. The hope of
Israel was fulfilled; the longed-for Messiah was
come, and was even then in the city of David.
Strange contrast! 'Twas but a Babe in a manger
that had set the angels hymning glory to God
in the highest. Then, as the heavenly vision with-
draws, the shepherds have but one thought, to
hurry to Bethlehem; and when they had found
the Infant and His parents, all that heard their
story marvelled, but many treasured up the
memory of it all, and pondered over it. And
the shepherds returned, praising and thanking
God for the vision and its fulfilment.

Other guests there were also, wise men from
the East, perhaps seers of Babylonia who had
studied the stars. For the Jews had been there
in captivity, and even now were in those parts
in large numbers, and might speak to the na-
tives of the star that should arise out of Jacob

(Numbers XXIV, 17). And a wondrous star they had indeed seen, and its meaning, we cannot doubt, had been revealed to them, for otherwise they would not have had the merit of faith. The King of the Jews was born! And what a trial to them when, after their long journey and all the difficulties they had overcome and the sneers against which they had doubtless to steel themselves, nothing was known of Him at Jerusalem! Terrified of Herod, the priests and scribes dared say no word; even when questioned by him, they dared show no interest, in spite of the tremendous excitement all around them. The Wise Men left the chosen city faithful, yet alone and disappointed. They had not needed the star to guide them to it, but now upon a sudden it flared out once more, to show them the very house they sought. Great their joy at beholding it, greater still in paying their homage to the Child and His Mother. Thus the gentiles were called by faith to worship the Infant Saviour, and present their choicest gifts. Long ago the Psalmist had exhorted all nations to praise the Lord (Psalm 116), and now they are beginning in earnest. And the God who brought them sends them back; their trust in Him is a surer protection than the wise terror of the high-priests and the scribes.

In our turn we kneel before the Babe Divine, and believe and adore and trust and love.

FIFTH DAY, SECOND MEDITATION:

THE TWO STANDARDS.

We have here the second great parable, if such we may call it, that St. Ignatius proposes. In the meditation on 'Christ the King' it was in the main the call of our Divine Leader in itself that we were considering. Now it is to be chiefly His plan of campaign, and, by way of contrast, the plan of campaign of His great adversary, the Devil. They are engaged in a great war, fighting for the souls of men. We have to realise, then, in the first place, that there is a war going on. Men may want to be left alone in peace, they may resent the zeal of other men who would arouse them to a sense of sin and judgment, and in general to their responsibilities. They may try to harden themselves against all possible disturbing influences. But they cannot hinder the one great central fact, that there *is* a worldwide warfare in progress, that they are being fought for, aye, and are fighting themselves. 'He that is not with me is against me'; every man is not merely himself a prize for Christ or the Devil, but is himself fighting on the side of the one or the other.

The *mise-en-scène*, to be worked out more elaborately afterwards, is twofold. By Jerusalem Christ marshals his followers, in a great field, and Satan his by Babylon. The cities chosen are the city of peace and the city of confusion. Our prayer is for knowledge of both leaders, and of their respective methods. Satan's wiles we desire to understand in order to beware of them, and we pray for help therein; but Christ offers us true life, the following and imitation of Himself, and we pray to make this indeed our life, our whole career and our whole being.

SATAN. We come, then, to consider Satan, upon a throne of fire and smoke, a terrible figure to behold. The fire may be taken to signify the devastation which he has wrought upon himself and upon others, and is scheming to work upon still more. We may also think of it as a punishment. Satan manages to impose upon the world, yet his relation to his foe, if such we may call Almighty God, is that of one undergoing a severe chastisement. His position is in reality full of ignominy; power he has in abundance, yet once again it is the Being whom he has made his enemy that must accord permission for its use. Else what hope had we? But God is faithful, and does not suffer us to be tempted above our strength, but bestows abundant grace and easy victory to them that call upon Him with humility and trust. In utter reliance on Him, we in our measure may have a part in His contempt of the renegade angel. The fire may thus remind us also of Satan's rage and frenzy; cunning is there, and yet a cunning that must often foil itself, because it lacks calm deliberation. In place of that, there is intolerable pain and many a fierce passion, a malice that cannot always be restrained, but sometimes defeats its own ends, when merciless torture itself drives the victim back to God. Thus we may find much meaning in the fire. And in the smoke thickly mingled therewith we may recognise the darkness in which Satan shrouds his work and his designs. The poor dupe must be kept in ignorance and perplexity, he must not be clear in his own mind, nor yet go to others for instruction and counsel. It is the children of the light who are safe, if any can be, they who leave no dark place in their soul, but desire to see and know themselves as God sees and knows them, and are not ashamed to call in one of His ministers to help them.

What is Satan doing? He is sending his devils everywhere, to every country, every town, every individual; none are too high, nor any too low for him. Every one is to be dragged down to hell that possibly can be; that is his mean revenge against His Creator for having cast him out of heaven, and His Creator allows him a certain measure of freedom therein, that men, too, may have their probation. And how is he addressing his subordinates? His language, we may be sure, is not instinct with tender charity;

nevertheless there is a definite plan of campaign which he proposes to all, and which they accept. They hate their seducer, but he is the most cunning of them, and can help them to their common design of evil.

According to St. Ignatius, the usual plan followed is this. First of all men are to be tempted to covet riches; thence they are to be brought to vainglory, and after that to great pride. Once so far, other vices can be superinduced without great difficulty.

At first sight this is a surprising doctrine, and does not seem true to the facts of human nature. What a number of souls, for example, are ruined by impurity! And yet there seems little room in the above scheme for a destructive vice of this kind; it appears to occupy too subordinate a place.

Now we must remember, in the first place, that St. Ignatius is not laying down a metaphysical axiom; his rule may not fit all. But experience shows that, if rightly understood, it fits most. There is question here, not of what one may call the predominant passion, but of the root vice that underlies them all and safeguards them against repentance. A man may be addicted to impurity, but the struggle against it will be lacking in earnestness according as these more fundamental failings have sapped his spiritual strength. There is question of the whole

bent of one's life, whether it be directed in the
main to God or to creatures. Riches represent
at bottom all that can be sought in the world
apart from God, and the power to enjoy creatures. Once we crave to 'have' for its own sake,
it is indeed, as the Apostle says, idolatry. No
doubt, the ordinary Christian may entertain a
lawful desire for riches; yet if Our Lord's words
in the Gospel mean anything, it is a desire that
is very unwise, for it makes the attainment of
heaven extremely difficult.

Riches are to lead to vainglory. The step is
easy; possession of things worth having leads
to a certain self-complacency, which is increased
by the deference which it receives from others.
The door is shut all the more firmly against a
return to God; man has then not only turned
to creatures, but is satisfied with them.

Pride is the climax, and the supreme bar to
repentance. The man has become more and more
pleased with himself, and other creatures feign
the same pleasure. No great wealth is needed
for all this, but only the possession of something that can yield satisfaction, and is recognised as such by others. But, so far as it
goes, God is dethroned, and self placed in His
stead. A man's whole attitude towards life becomes one ghastly delusion. Any sin may come
then, and with his whole spiritual fabric under-
mined, the sinner will be at its mercy. The

ordinary motives for repentance will have lost all meaning.

CHRIST. And now we turn to Christ, who stands, lovely and lovable, amid His followers, without any kind of external display. He, too, makes choice of many, and despatches them throughout the world to help mankind, and win them for Himself. There are, of course, His holy angels, but it is scarcely to our present purpose to dwell upon them. Let us salute these blessed beings with reverence, and beg them to help us with their prayers, that we may be at once their conquest and their allies.

What is the plan of campaign of Christ's servants? It is diametrically opposite to the Devil's. First of all Christ would have them bring all to spiritual poverty, to detachment from creatures. Nay, they should be ready even for actual poverty, should it please the Divine Majesty to call them to that. This is the beginning of a turning away from creatures, and a casting of oneself upon God: it means a loss of all interest in creatures, save in so far as God can be loved in them, and they in God. It is therefore a great safeguard even against the sins which it does not directly attack; as long as it is retained, there is always an easy path to repentance. And this persevering love of spiritual, and even actual poverty is apt to lead both to silent and to outspoken contempt, because he who possesses

it is hopelessly wanting in all that the world
esteems and strives after. When, therefore, a
man has come to welcome this contempt as part
of Christ's plan of campaign, and as detaching
him still further from creatures, and attaching
him to the Creator, then he has made another
great stride forward, and he is near his goal,
humility. He will come easily to understand
that nothing comes to him from himself, but
all from God; he will find no difficulty in abase-
ment, since in himself he finds naught but evil.
Thus he will be ready to fight beneath Christ's
standard as His true follower, and to model himself upon his crucified Lord.

And now once more, as in the meditation on
Christ the King, let us remind ourselves that
the work here proposed to us has an apostolic
aspect, none the less real if it is not urged on
us directly. In the first place we are to look to
ourselves; nothing can excuse us from that. But
the fact still remains that Christ is endeavouring
to win all mankind, and that these are the principles which St. Ignatius represents Him as pro-
pounding to His servants, not primarily to practise, but to preach. It is only in the immediate
application that St. Ignatius speaks merely of practice, and that because of its supreme importance
to the individual, whether he is called upon to
preach or no. Yet few are those to whom it
should not fall in some way or another to preach

these principles. In all work for souls, and even in all their intercourse, religious should show forth the poverty and humility of Christ, and all the beatitudes, not merely in deed, though in a manner that is the most important, but also in thought and word. There is a certain danger sometimes that unconsciously they may almost come to have two standards, one for themselves and one for those in the world, and while practising poverty themselves, pay unworthy homage to the possessors of wealth. Yet, if the Gospel means anything, it is not these latter who are the fortunate ones of the earth, and it is not their condition that can be put before others as the supreme ideal. Best of all, where it is reasonably possible, is renunciation; and after that complete detachment, and generosity to God and His poor. Thus the heart of the religious must be truly in his poverty, so as to make him the apostle thereof; and also so as to make it for him the true path to humility. To cling fast to poverty means to disregard the esteem of the world, and in the long run to abjure one's esteem of self, to be ready for humiliations, to nail oneself to the cross of Christ, to claim naught, to crave naught, save the love that never dies, that love for Him which He alone can give.

These thoughts will be more fully understood as the retreat progresses. For the present, we make that triple prayer which St. Ignatius re-

serves for the more important meditations, first
to Our Lady, that she may obtain us the special
grace, whatever in any particular meditation it
may be, from her Son: then to the Son, that
He obtain it from the Father: then to the Father
Himself, that He grant it. And here our prayer
is, that we be received under Christ's standard,
in absolute poverty of spirit, and even in actual
poverty, in whatever form He will; further, in
endurance of affronts and injuries, for the further
imitation of Him, and provided there be no sin,
or displeasure of the Divine Majesty. Having
thus accepted Christ once more, with increased
loyalty and understanding, for our only Leader
and Eternal King, we return to the contemplation of His life, to draw thence yet more light
and more love.

FIFTH DAY, CONSIDERATION:

THE TRIPLE CORD.

As we near the end of our retreat, we seem
to understand more clearly the spiritual ideals
which we are proposing to ourselves. It may
help matters if we now attempt to sum them up
in a single formula, and at the same time endeavour
to sum up the perfect religious as a whole, taking
into account what appear to be the two chief
traits which, while they are not perhaps a necessary constituent of virtue, at all events not

necessary if considered in their widest extent, must none the less form part of the equipment of the religious today, if he is to exercise any kind of influence over others. 'A threefold cord is not easily broken', says Ecclesiastes; the perfectly equipped religious is a gentleman, a scholar, and a saint.

GENTLEMAN. Many a man would think it the most natural thing in the world that a priest, or even other people, should in some way or another imply that he has been guilty of sins and imperfections, but will bridle up at once if the imputation be cast upon him that he is not a perfect gentleman. For religious it is an unworthy thing to yield to such pique or vanity, and they will be prepared, in this as in other matters, to consider carefully what is the ideal that they ought to put before themselves, and in what respect and to what extent they fall short of it. Nor, indeed, is it surprising that this point should occasionally need looking to. Many religious come to the noviceship more or less straight from school, and a certain amount that might be picked up in the course of home life, has to be picked up in religion instead, under circumstances in some respects less favourable — by no means in all respects, for an ungainly fault is sometimes cured in a few weeks that otherwise would have remained for life.

What then is meant by being a gentleman?
Perhaps, after all, the simplest solution is best,
and we may call him 'a gentle man'. It is not
'gentle' to thunder down stairs three at a time in
heavy boots, to bang doors, to tread on people's
heels, to break a large proportion of the objects
with which one comes into contact. And again,
a loud and rough manner in speaking, and still
more in eating, or, to stretch matters a little
further, any notable lack of neatness and cleanliness — all these things, and others like them,
evidently call for a remedy. And to outward
gentleness corresponds gentleness of soul, consideration and sympathy with others, even where
they may be to some extent at fault; at times,
no doubt, severity may be needed towards those
in one's charge, but real harshness offends Almighty God no less than it displeases man. From
a gentleman, too, a certain refinement is expected
which is less directly connected with gentleness,
though it may be said naturally to flow from it;
a passable pronunciation of his native language
and a reasonable acquaintance with its literature,
perhaps even a certain amount in the way of
personal accomplishments, which can do so much
to further apostolic work, at home no less than
on the missions; some power of conversation and
self-expression, based upon general reading, personal experience, and the like; and finally, not
to go into the matter at length, some familiarity

with the usual amenities of life. For the sake
of apostolic work one should aim at being able
to get on well with people of the world, for it
is not always the poor with whom we have to
deal, and others can often do more for the
Kingdom of God, if they will. Nay, there is
an art, though a simpler one, even in making
friends with the poor. Virtue in itself is not
enough, but virtue must stimulate the religious
to make up what may be lacking in this part of
his equipment. Tact is invaluable, but not so
easily learnt; at all events we can say in general
that a little care and reflection about all these
things is sure to make a considerable difference
in the long run. It is well to remember that
in these matters proficiency in athletics is of no
avail, nor even the regular fulfilment of religious
duties; even the possession of what is essential
does not excuse from what is of lesser moment,
but is rather a stimulus to the attaining of it.

Nevertheless a true religious spirit is of enormous help in all that is recognised as essential
to a gentleman, not merely from the fact that
the religious is accustomed to make an effort to
correct his faults, but because he is bound to
cultivate the spirit which is recognised to be the
mainspring of a gentleman's thought and action.
He may be a little puzzled when he has green
things and red things and yellow things offered
him for his refreshment, and wonder whether

11 *

knife or spoon or fingers offer the most becoming
means of attack; after all, it is not always edifying
to be so very well versed in the manipulation of
such viands, alien as they are to the frugal life of
religious. Nor is it always possible for a religious
to conform to the etiquette which governs social
relations in the world outside; and in any case
he may find it difficult to learn a code to which
his ordinary life is not wholly subject. But in
effacing himself, in mortification, in charity, he
should be well versed, and these naturally express
themselves in perfect gentleness.

SCHOLAR. Clearly it is only by using the
word in a very wide sense that we can speak
of obligations of scholarship as incumbent upon
all religious. Yet it is worth while to insist upon
the store of sheer knowledge, and accurate knowledge, that they ought to possess. In the first
place, for their own spiritual good; for it is the
chief business of their lives to think upon the
great truths of religion, so as to become the very
embodiment of those truths in thought and will
and action — a thing which it is impossible for
them to do, if they have nothing but a perverted
or substantially inadequate notion of what those
truths are. No doubt Almighty God can grant
an intense realisation of the great dogmas even
to those to whom they are little better than
disiecta membra, but such is not the ordinary
course of His Providence. And while we are

on this subject, it may be worth while to reflect how much good is left undone by those who devote no time or care to solid instruction in the retreats which they give to religious. What they say should be inspired throughout by Catholic dogma, for otherwise it will certainly lack solidity; and it is better that such a background should be clearly perceived. And there are points which are not immediately dogmatic on which they can give very useful instruction, such as the nature and obligations of religious life; and, in general, there is much of this nature which religious should know.

So much for the knowledge which a religious may be said to need for his own sake. The knowledge which he will need for the sake of others may be summed up under three heads, namely, the knowledge required by priests, the knowledge required by teachers, and the knowledge required by all for instruction and ordinary intercourse. The equipment of priests as such does not fall within our scope, and we may be content with one or two passing remarks. The enemies of the Church realise, better perhaps than her children, the importance of erudition in moulding the thoughts of nations, and they have been only too successful in excluding loyal Catholics from chairs in the important universities of Europe. The Church, therefore, must rely to a large extent on work done with inadequate means and amid hostile criticism and sometimes bigoted opposition — work of an uphill kind that must largely be undertaken by religious if it is to be done at all. 'Speaking and preaching', as Mrs. Benson wrote to Hugh[1], 'are more *insistent*, and require less faith.' The need of more good Catholic literature is great; and even in literature itself there are kinds of writing that 'are more insistent and require less faith'. Yet a multitude of machine-guns is not sufficient to cope with the heavy artillery of the enemy, and the big books and the important lectures on the wrong side certainly need experts carefully trained in right views to cope with them. These, however, are considerations which more concern superiors than subjects. Priestly work of the ordinary pastoral kind chiefly demands accurate knowledge in the pulpit and in the confessional. There is great need that in the former the whole of our faith should be clearly set forth, not merely for the sake of Catholics, but also of non-Catholics, who in the present state of religious unrest are often glad to profit by such exposition. On the knowledge required in the confessional it is not necessary to dwell; evidently great mischief may follow if the priest be incapable. Then there are retreats to be considered, and spiritual direction

---

[1] *The Life of Mgr. R. H. Benson*, by C. C. Martindale, S. J., vol. II, p. 122.

generally, which demand a certain religious experience and ascetical training.   Ordinary and extraordinary confessors to religious communities may do a great work for God if they take their duties seriously, endeavouring both to secure the requisite knowledge and to use it.

The teacher must obviously know what is to be taught, and should know a great deal more of the subject besides.   There is danger of dry rot within, from an indiscreet zeal for immediate results; time may be devoted to individual pupils that were best spent in mastering the subject to be taught, in advancing in it, in learning how to teach, in doing other things the practical results of which are less obvious.   It is not a laudable zeal, but a grave delusion, that leads one to be always giving out knowledge without oneself taking in any fresh supply.   And, needless to say, the most important subject to be taught is religious doctrine.   There is only too much danger of its being elbowed out by the pressure of examinations, yet there never was a time when it was more necessary, both because one may find objections to Christianity and Catholicism brought up, or rather presupposed, in any halfpenny paper, and because many are genuinely anxious to know what Catholics have to say for themselves, and to give it a fair hearing. Evidently, as has already been said, this religious instruction should include the outlines of Holy Scripture and

Church History. Children also need a certain amount of instruction about the things of the body; elementary notions of hygiene and the like, not excluding first aid. Nowadays it is an elementary safeguard to their morality not to let them leave school without sufficient instruction on sexual questions; how this is best given is a disputed question, but one way that has been found successful is to make it incidental to an explanation of the virginal motherhood of Our Blessed Lady. It is also possible to lead up to it through botany and biology.

We have been speaking of the acquisition and retention of knowledge; and it is natural to add a few words on the subject of libraries, without which the acquisition and retention of knowledge is practically impossible. Two things are needed to make a library serviceable, a fixed allowance and a policy; the amount of money to be spent should not be left to whim or circumstance, and still less the spending of it. Again, where many are living together, the proper use of the library becomes very important; books should not be taken out unless with due entry of the fact, or be kept out longer than they are needed. This is not an obligation of poverty, chastity and obedience, but of poverty, charity and obedience. And it may be added that a library needs careful looking after, a duty, like other duties, best performed when it is a labour of love.

SAINT. This aspect or strand of the triple cord needs but few words, since the whole retreat is concerned with it; but it may be useful, as we have said, to attempt to sum it up in a single formula, and that the key to the whole thought of St. Paul. ''Tis no longer I that live, 'tis Christ liveth in me' (Gal. II, 20). There is the negative side to holiness, the element in us that must live no more, that must be crucified upon the cross of Christ; and there is the positive side, our union with Christ through prayer and grace and sacrament, that is ever capable of fresh strength and development. Therefore mortification is necessary, the stern repression of our lower inclinations, even the welcoming and quest of much from which nature shrinks; but this is not because there is any value in suffering taken in itself, but because it can be used to give Christ fuller possession of our hearts and souls. If we rid ourselves of unworthy affections, it is not in order to create a void within ourselves, but in order to make ampler room for our Divine Lover. Nor again does this mean that everything that is natural is to disappear, but only what opposes or impedes the supernatural. Natural gifts, for example, are often of immense value in the service of God, and in that case are to be used to the full, but affection towards them must be purified. In short, there is that in us which must live no more, but it is only that which hinders Christ from living in us, and from taking full possession of us; and only in so far as it does so. But to Christ's life and rule within us we must allow no limit, or to what we believe He can accomplish in us. It is want of confidence in Him and in His love that is the great reason why souls do not advance.

FIFTH DAY, THIRD MEDITATION:

THE HOLY FAMILY.

In the first meditation today we have contemplated the Nativity, and in the first tomorrow we shall attempt to realise the dominating principles of the public ministry. The present exercise may be said to embrace all the time that intervenes, but here also we shall endeavour to look for characteristic features of the time rather than follow such events as we know to have happened. These latter can be worked out during the year, but of course any that prefer may fall back on them at once.

THE WORLD. We may consider the members of the Holy Family first in their relation to the world outside, next in their relations with each other, finally in their relation to God. If we consider their relations with the world outside first, the most astonishing and significant fact is, that the life of the Holy Family was indeed a hidden one, the life of persons of little importance

in a town of little importance. We have to bring
home to ourselves that day after day went by,
and year after year, even after Our Blessed Lord
was well past twenty, and still no attempt to
evangelise either Jew or Gentile. How differently,
if we may say so reverently, would Christ have
been run by the modern astute manager! Nay,
if we look at the matter as even the best of
men might be tempted to look at it, how many
chances gone of teaching and helping both the
native and them that were from afar! And what
we have said of Christ would apply, though in
a far lesser degree, to Our Blessed Lady, and also
to St. Joseph. Never, it might be thought,
was there a more terrible example of a light
being hid under a bushel.

We may doubtless assume that nothing but
the gravest reasons would have kept Our Lord
with His parents in their hidden life. It was
for our instruction, to teach us not to judge
these matters by mere worldly standards. There
are two chief lessons to be learnt: in the first
place, the need of preparation for our work,
and then the love of the hidden life in itself.
The world hates the latter and scamps the
former. Yet much preparation is necessary, both
for religious in general and still more for such
as are to be priests, if they wish to do solid
work for God. What is supremely necessary is
training in the paths of virtue — to walk aright

oneself and to be in one's measure a reliable guide. Nothing can possibly be of greater service in this direction than a fervent retreat; it is obviously this that most helps the religious himself, and it is his own experience of himself that will always afford the best foundation for guidance of others, though it needs to be supplemented by experience of others also, and the consultation of good authorities — whether by actual intercourse or reading. Then there is a more distinctly professional training; the training of an efficient nurse or teacher, and most of all of an efficient priest, is a long and arduous business, and there is always a longing and a temptation to be up and doing, to put into practice at once what little we have already mastered (or think we have mastered), and in consequence to be content for the rest of our lives with mediocrity. Christ was thinking of all this in those long and useless years of waiting! If the angels could weep, what floods of tears would they not have shed over the neglect of His lesson! How soon the Corinthians thought they could get on well enough without a Paul to train them! 'Already ye have had your fill! Already ye are rich! Ye have come to reign without us! And would that ye did indeed reign, that we too might reign with you!' (I Cor. IV, 8.)

But it is not only when in process of formation that we need to keep the hidden life of Christ

before us; to love the cross is at all times to
love to be hidden and unknown, and at all times
love for the Creator draws the soul powerfully
away from creatures to Himself, so that it is
a pain to turn to them once more. 'Love to be
unknown', says the Imitation (I, 2, 3), and again,
'No one is safe in coming forward, who does
not gladly remain in obscurity' (I, 20, 2). If we
truly abhor honour and the spirit of the world,
we must necessarily abhor appearing in the lime-
light. And for the most part truly solid work
for God, the best work that most of us can do,
is obscure work, and a craving for publicity
may do much to endanger it. Still, publicity
in itself is a thing indifferent, and in some kinds
of work is the almost inevitable accompaniment
of efficient zeal for God. If, therefore, a good
opening presents itself, the possibility that he
may make a little noise in the world should in
no wise deter an apostle, but he should strike
out boldly, knowing well that His Divine Leader
will give him ample grace to save his head from
being turned, even as it is more than enough
to deliver him from every other danger.

FAMILY LIFE. We need to make ourselves
at home with the Holy Family, to think the
thoughts of that Family, and in our measure
to lead its life. The Holy Family is more directly a model for Christian families, and we shall
do well to propose it as such. It is important

nowadays to defend the home both against the direct assault of an immoral propaganda and against the more insidious attack of the modern bureaucracy, which robs the parent of all proper responsibility. The home needs to be strengthened in every right and practicable way; even girls of the better classes, for example, are taught little enough that is likely to make a good wife or mother. Such arts and such family life may be esteemed lightly only when there is question of renouncing them for Christ. But the supernatural family, the religious community, has also much to learn from Jesus, Mary and Joseph. True, in the second meditation of the fourth day we accepted Christ for our Divine Captain, and from that meditation, and from the consideration on obedience, we can readily understand how much there is in the military spirit that we can with profit make our own — the dash and loyalty, the steady endurance in training and in action. But even an army should be, in the words of the poet, a band of brothers; and in any case we can see without further ado that a family spirit should indeed reign in a religious house. We who live together in the common service of Christ should feel a family love for each other, a family interest in each other, a family regard for the good name of each member thereof, a family readiness to overlook each other's failings and to bear one another's burdens. And this family spirit should extend to other members of the house, and most of all to children under our care, if such there be; the religious should be in very truth their fathers and their big brothers. That is the only education that can be called Christian; indeed, it is not education at all to watch boys fight their own battle, to leave it to chance and their own immature natures whether they sink or swim.

Viewed even from a merely human standpoint, and abstracting in so far as we may need to do so from the infinite perfection of Our Blessed Lord, the members of the Holy Family might be said to have given each other no ground for complaint; with us, poor human nature does not go so far, but we may learn from the consideration of the Holy Family much that will help us not to give and not to take offence, much that will promote concord and love. Cheerfulness and charity we need; both a readiness to give practical help, and a horror of all that savours of gloom or sourness. Truly to bear one another's burdens means all this and more; it is to help others both in deed and look and word. It also means putting up with their failings, such as they are, and a consciousness that one is not without them oneself; a charity based on the presupposition that all are to be perfect is not worth the ink that writes it. Rather let us ponder again and again the magnificent panegyric

of charity in I Cor. XIII, and the strong warnings
uttered by Our Lord against judging our fellows.
Even for His executioners He could plead that
they knew not what they did. Malice, needless to
say, or anything remotely approaching revenge,
a desire to take another down, often enough
even the desire to resist evil, are contrary to
that supreme law of charity; a religious' best
friends should be those of his own community,
and it is in his own community that his best
apostolic work should be done. Certainly life
should not be made a trial, as for example
thoughtless teasing may make it, to those who
bear the burden and the heat of the day; they
should find their joy and their strength in their
brethren — a joy and a strength that to be spiritual must be based on a frank recognition of
the claims of God. If low standards be perpetually taken for granted in conversation, even
though it be but in jest, they react upon the
soul. Indeed, practically every religious tends
to raise or lower the standard, and some religious
very much so; scandal and good example are
present in every human society, and extend to
small things no less than great. One should
also observe the ancient saying, 'Be not a lion
in the house', which is a good enough precept
in its modern sense, though Ben Sirach meant
it more literally. In the matter of intercourse,
as in the matter of food, it is better to lean to

what is simple and solid and wholesome, rather than to what is more fascinating but a little dangerous.

Lay-brothers may learn from the Holy Family to esteem manual work and the especial virtues that should accompany it, to be ready and willing workers, even when there is extra work to be done, as at times there must be, and yet all the while to value their spiritual life and their spiritual duties. We may all learn to care for the old and the sick, as St. Joseph was cared for, and for children, who should represent to us Our Blessed Lord. We learn, too, how to command and how to obey; to the Divine Child we naturally entrust our vow of obedience, to His Virgin-Mother our chastity, to St. Joseph our poverty.

GOD. The hidden life was a time of recollection and prayer, and it was that, simply because God wished it so to be. As we have already seen, it is a mistake to pour ourselves out upon external work, and to think that the only practical service we can render God. We may be called to work zealously at the outward ministry; on the other hand, we may not. In any case, the most practical service we can render Almighty God is to work unremittingly at our own perfection.

And that perfection consists in the perfect union of our own will with the will of God.

We see this in the Holy Family, not merely in such trials as the flight into Egypt or the death, whenever it took place, of St. Joseph, but in their constant daily life. They were not longing for ampler scope or greater display. In the same way religious have a work to do, and should perform it as perfectly as possible, not aiming at ulterior possibilities, except at the wish or with the approval of superiors, and with a desire to be quit of all false ambition. Dreams of the future too easily mar the present, even where there is a duty of actual training and preparation.

In loving their Jesus, Mary and Joseph loved God. That is the value of the personal love of Christ; God took flesh to win our love, and by loving what we can, as it were, see and touch and hear, we love God Himself. We must not consider our love of God and our love of the God-man as two distinct things.

One more lesson; Jesus tarried in the Temple to teach all parents that the claims of God are paramount. And there is no greater reward for the parents' virtue than a call to the child to follow Christ more perfectly in the way of the counsels.

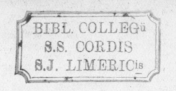
SIXTH DAY.

THE HOLY EUCHARIST.

PATRON: St. John the Evangelist.

READING: Mark XIV; I Cor. X; XI, 17-34; Imitation IV, 2, 17.

FIRST MEDITATION: The Public Ministry (Human Suffering, Divine Power, Incarnate Love).

SECOND MEDITATION: The Holy Eucharist (The Sacrifice [1], The Sacrament, The Abiding Presence).

CONSIDERATION: Poverty (The Vow, The Virtue, The Practice).

THIRD MEDITATION: The Sacred Heart (The Appeal, Our Answer, The First Friday).

✝

---

[1] For Père de la Taille's doctrine of the Sacrifice, see his brilliant lecture at the Summer School of Catholic Studies at Cambridge, printed in *Catholic Faith in the Holy Eucharist*, edited by the present writer (Cambridge, 1923). His monumental work, *Mysterium Fidei*, appeared too late for notice here

12 *

THE HOLY EUCHARIST.

Now Thou art lifted high
In sacrifice, and we prepare
Thy Cross to share;
Now let the old Adam die,
And all that is not Thee, Lord, crucify!

Now Thou art nurture blest,
Possessing where Thou art possessed;
Our life be Thine,
Thought, word and deed Divine:
Cast all away, save what Thou hallowest!

We go; but night and day
Thou, in Thy tabernacled stay
Biddest return,
Utterly there to burn
In Eucharistic life and love away!

SIXTH DAY, FIRST MEDITATION:

THE PUBLIC MINISTRY.

IT would be easy to make choice of some particular scene or scenes from the public life of Our Blessed Lord for our contemplation. That is what we do during the year, and there is always plenty of fruit to be drawn from individual incidents. But it may be more useful for the purposes of retreat rather to fix our standpoint, to grasp the main features which characterised Our Lord's ministry throughout. We may contemplate them also in all their agelong significance, as reflected in the life of His Mystical Body, the Church, and according to our measure in our own. This will help us to see our work in a true perspective, as a manifestation of the divine life of the Church, and of Christ working through her; and thus we shall come to attune our souls more perfectly to the strategy of our Leader, which we have spent some meditations in endeavouring to master. The detailed contemplation of the public life will occupy many a meditation during the year, and it is to be hoped, will be helped by the light acquired in the present exercise, which itself can, of course, be repeated and developed.

HUMAN SUFFERING. No one needs to be told that the life of Our Lord ended in great suffering, but not all realise that this was but the

climax to what had just preceeded, and indeed
was foreshadowed by all the distress of His in-
fancy. Of the hidden life we know too little
to speak, but the lesson of that life lies precisely in its hidden character; on the one hand
it doubtless had its troubles, on the other hand
it was not perhaps in the Divine plan that suffering should at this stage attain to the intensity
which it reached later, even before the passion.
The lesson of the hidden life is rather the need
of quiet and prayerful preparation. But when
the ministry begins, we find immense and thank-
less labours, hardships both for Our Lord's sacred Body and for His Soul. No doubt He had
a home at Capharnaum, but He was often away
from it, either evangelising Galilee in general or
working beyond its confines. When finally departing from Galilee He declared: 'The Son of
Man hath not where to lay His Head' (Luke
IX, 58); and this was frequently His condition
before then. He was likewise at times without
food; at times the common purse sufficed to buy
supplies (John IV, 8), but at times (e. g. Mark
III, 20) the very attraction of His preaching made
it impossible to have a meal, while such an incident as the plucking of the ears of corn (Mark
II, 23, etc.) really does suggest a shortage. Nor
did He spare himself fatigue. He sat down tired
at the well near Sychar (John IV, 6); He invited
His disciples to come and rest awhile (Mark

VI, 31), but in actual fact their departure by
boat only ended in more teaching, and in the
multiplication of the loaves, and all that followed.
And how much more is needed to complete the
tale of suffering! His enemies were ever among
His audience, looking for something that they
might distort into an accusation against Him;
and what could be more disheartening than the
presence of such slanderers? Disciples, too,
proved dull and weak; what more encouraging
to a teacher than the quick and zealous learner?
Christ was the great failure; and His passion and
death were only the climax to what was already
tragedy.

And His Church leads a crucified life also,
nailed to His cross. How can we even pretend
to estimate the measure of her sufferings? Her
labours are immense, the work of so many who
even in the world give, not only of their money
and of their goods, but, best of all, of their own
service to God and their neighbour — the work,
too, of those who consecrate their whole lives to
Christ without reserve. How little noise they
make, and yet how great fruit they bear! And
there are dangers and difficulties and discourage-
ments without number, known only to themselves
and the angels. Among the greatest sufferings
of the Church is persecution, and not least a
more or less covert persecution from governments
professing to be Catholic. And there are false

children and scandals, and calumnies where scandals fail. The Church, too, is of all failures the most colossal.

And we have a share in this suffering; let us not hide it from ourselves, but be grateful that we have a part in Christ and His mystical Spouse. We have work to do, disappointments to bear, persecution, calumnies, failures. Let us set Christ before us, and His glorious apostle. 'To this very hour we hunger and thirst and are naked and are buffeted, we are homeless and we toil, working with our own hands. We are reviled and we bless, we are persecuted and we endure, we are defamed and we answer softly; we have become as the refuse of the world, the offscouring of all men, even to this hour' (I Cor. IV, 11-13).

DIVINE POWER. That is one aspect of Christ's work, in Himself and in His Church and in us. Now let us look at the opposite side, at the Divine power which we everywhere see displayed. 'Never man spake thus'; it was not merely that he spoke with authority, differing in this from the scribes, but His doctrine and His manner of delivering it alike had an irresistible attraction for the multitude. The measure of His enemies' iniquity can be estimated by the difficulty they experience in bringing the populace round to their side. Nor was this the only manifestation of Christ's divine power. His human birth was

announced by an angel host, His ministry abound-
ed in miracles. His resurrection after death was
the greatest of all.

We have seen that the Church, too, is a colossal failure; she is also a most brilliant success,
a marvellous illustration of the persistent working
of God's power. We shall perhaps see this best
if we consider the four marks by which she is
and ever will be known; and if in connection
with these we recall the three powers left by
Christ with His Church, the power to teach, the
power to govern, and the power of the ministry
or of the sacraments, the power, that is, of
direct sanctification. These powers are treated
of more at large in the third meditation of the
eighth day; there is no need to explain them at
length here. The unity of the Church, then,
chiefly refers to her government; in an age
hysterical with democracy her millions obey their
pastors, and most of all the supreme pastor, the
Vicar of Jesus Christ. At a time when we are
having it dinned into our ears that all are to
believe what they choose, without having in any
way to answer for it, the Church exacts ex-
plicit faith in a large body of doctrine — and
that faith is given. She has also a unity of
sacrament and sacrifice, but that would not of
itself suffice to make her truly but one corpo-
rate institution. Then, she is holy, holy in her
doctrine both as to faith and morals, holy in

her sacraments and other means of grace, holy
in her government and in the sanctity of her
children resulting from it. We see this in the
life of zeal and self-sacrifice led, not merely by
priests and religious, but by so many of the
laity; and also in many institutions which flourish
upon alms and personal service. We see Christ's
divine power also in the catholicity of the Church;
her unity would not be so wonderful if she did
not extend to all times and places, the only
really universal communion that there is. And
her universality in time means that she goes back
to the apostles, and to Our Blessed Lord.

'By the grace of God', says the Apostle, 'I am
what I am' (I Cor. xv, 10). We, too, must
acknowledge gratefully the working of His grace
in us; to it we owe all the good that we have
ever accomplished, through its powerful aid we
remain in God's friendship, and overcome the
many difficulties that beset our path. 'He that
boasteth, let him boast in the Lord' (II Cor. x, 17).
Whatever least particle of good there may have
been in our lives, whatever there may be in the
future, it gives us no cause to boast of ourselves, but indeed to boast of our God and His
power. And however much any one may have
accomplished in his life, even though it be as
much as the Apostle Paul, it is all the more
ground to be proud of our God, but never of
ourselves.

INCARNATE LOVE. And so to the solution of the mystery. For surely it is a mystery, this blending of unspeakable suffering with unlimited power. Though, indeed, we have seen something of the solution already, and shall see more as we proceed in the retreat. This, however, we may say now, that the true solution is love. Love ever expresses itself in suffering, and the Divine Lover of our souls did not choose, as He might have done, to remain an exception to this rule. For it was good for us that He should suffer. If we consider the sacrifice of Calvary, that, of course, meant our redemption. But even if we confine ourselves to the ministry, we can still see another reason. A life of suffering was the best thing He had to show us, the best life for us also to lead. Our own pleasure, our own honour, all the hundred and one things that allure us away from Him, all these lose their hold upon him who loves the cross of Christ, who loves Christ upon His cross.

The Church of Christ thus herself shows forth, not merely the suffering and the power, but also the love of her Divine Spouse. For He had nothing better to give her, out of the excess of His love, than His own cross. It was the best He had for her, both corporately and in her several members, that she and they might be the closer united to Him, the more effectively detached from the pleasures and honours of the world. And with the cross He gave the love that alone could bear it. It is the love of Christ that crucifies us to the world, to the better accomplishing of our own salvation and perfection; it is the love of Him that empowers us to toil and sacrifice ourselves, and enlist for Him others also. He may give us a heavy cross, but that is all the greater gift, because of the vast love with which He would suffuse our souls, and which would sweeten His yoke and lighten His burden. Let us be rid of every lesser thing than Himself, and in His own glad company, in intimate union with Him, let our ministry be the fellowship of His sufferings and our life a throb, not merely of love for Him, but of His own unfathomable love for man.

SIXTH DAY, SECOND MEDITATION:

THE HOLY EUCHARIST.

The Last Supper introduces us to the Passion. It contains several striking incidents, but none that can compare with the institution of the Holy Eucharist. We may treat the Supper historically if we will, from the moment that Christ enters the chosen house to the moment when He leaves it; but it has seemed more profitable to speak here only of the Blessed Sacrament. This latter must needs play an immense part in the life of every religious, and it would be a poor retreat that did not increase our devotion thereto, and our understanding of the great mysteries involved. The scene of this contemplation, then, will be Christ consecrating the sacred species and communicating His apostles; but the contemplation itself will deal with the Holy Eucharist as such, and chiefly in its three main aspects, Christ our Sacrifice, Christ our Food, Christ our Emmanuel, ever dwelling amongst us upon our altars.

THE SACRIFICE. Christ, at table with His apostles the night that His sufferings were to begin, is not afraid or ashamed of what is to befall. Rather He might almost be said to gloat over it. His friend is to betray Him, Jew and Gentile are to put Him to death after horrible torture; yet His one anxiety is, not that man should forget all this, but that it should be remembered, and He takes ample means to that effect. He knows that this hideous death will be understood by multitudes to be not merely a bewildering proof of love, but the greatest imaginable benefit. From the Cross is to flow out to them a ceaseless stream of graces; and the Crucified is not merely to be to them justness and sanctification and redemption (I Cor. I, 30), but also the model of their own lives. The tragedy of Calvary, therefore, is to be renewed, though in an unbloody manner; once more Mary stands beneath the Cross of her Son, and the beloved disciple beholds the blood and water flow from His side. The Body and Blood are mystically sundered by the words of consecration, which directly speak only of the bread becoming the Body and the wine the Blood. They are represented as apart, in a mystical renewal of that physical shedding of His Blood which Christ suffered on Calvary; and in that mystical shedding, according to a very common opinion, we have the reason why, as our Faith in any case teaches us, the Mass itself is a true sacrifice, though a sacrifice essentially commemorative of that of Calvary. In this way the death of the Lord is proclaimed, until He come (I Cor. XI, 26), even as Christ Himself proclaimed it before it came to pass. In this way the elevation at Holy Mass brings us daily to the foot of the Cross, and we have to think, not merely of the Real Presence which the words of consecration effect, but of the sacrificed state in which they bring Christ before us. And it is Christ sacrificed, with Christ for sacrificer; it is in reality He who offers Himself up, the priest merely speaking in His person. In a word, all the thoughts with which the sacrifice of Calvary may inspire us find their place in our consideration of the sacrifice of the Mass. But it is not merely our own thoughts that profit us, but virtue goes out from the sacrifice itself to us. As the Council of Trent declares, 'the Lord, appeased by this offering, granteth grace and the gift of repentance, forgiving even huge crimes and sins' (Session XXII, chap. 2); much more therefore will He be ready to bestow His graces upon those who through His mercy stand in His grace. For even so the Apostle, writing to those who had been converted in adult age, argues that if Christ died for them when they were sinners, much more, now that they are justified through His Blood, will He save them from the divine anger (Rom. V, 8-9).

And now, as the Apostle also says, 'they that are Christ's have crucified their flesh, with its vices and concupiscences' (Gal. V, 24). We have also to crucify ourselves, and to remain crucified upon our cross. We have to resist the allurement of sin, even, so far as with God's grace we can, of venial sin; and that alone will cost us not a little. To serve God more perfectly we have to sacrifice more; the more we die to ourselves, the more we live and work for Him. We need therefore, to offer ourselves up as Christ's fellow-victims, or rather, to offer ourselves in and with Him, since, as the Apostle yet again says, we must be one with Him in His death (cf. Rom. VI, 5 : Philip. III, 10). In such a spirit let us assist at the sacrifice upon our altars, so to drink in deepest meaning and deepest grace for ourselves.

THE SACRAMENT. It was pointed out in the Consideration for the fifth day, that there is a negative and a positive side to holiness; there is the repression of evil and the increase in grace,

the death of the old Adam and the life of the
new man in Christ. Now it is to the negative
side in the main that belongs that sacrifice of
ourselves which we have just been considering,
that immolating of self in the mystical immolation
of the Lamb that was slain from the beginning.
But this death of the merely natural man, so far
as he cannot be transformed, this mortification
and renunciation, is not an end in itself, for
indeed, we have already seen that it is to be made
in and with Christ. In this way we appropriate
the virtue and merits of Christ's death, and so
live with Him in new life. With Him we die to
sin; with Him we live to God. This Christ-life is
grace, the transformation of the soul by sanctifying
grace, the constant energising of it by actual
grace. This is our spiritual life, the positive side
of sanctity; and of this spiritual life the Holy
Eucharist as a sacrament is the food.

Every sacrament is an outward sign of inward
grace. In Baptism the outward sign is that of
washing away, but the washing away is an inward
grace, it is primarily original sin that is to be
washed away. And the outward sign of the
Holy Eucharist is the sign of food or nutrition,
it is the appearance of bread and wine, of the
ordinary food and drink of Christ's time and
country, and indeed of many other countries in
all times. But it is not the mere nutrition of
the body that Christ intended; this outward sign

of food symbolises the nutrition, the feeding of the soul, such as Christ explained it in John VI. 'Except you eat the flesh of the Son of man, and drink his blood, you shall not have (or, according to the Greek, you have not) life in you' (John VI, 54). The Holy Eucharist, therefore, is to discharge the function of food to the soul. It is not a medicine, restoring us to health when sick, for that is the function proper to the sacrament of Penance; nor again is it a luxury for special occasions, or a reward for exceptional virtue. It is to be our ordinary, frequent, daily food, maintaining, and even increasing, the vigour of our spiritual life, helping us to resist all noxious influences and their evil after-effects, and to advance in all virtue. It was on these lines that Pope Pius X settled the doubts and difficulties that existed on the subject of frequent Communion; and in the new Code of Canon Law it is laid down that the faithful are to be exhorted to frequent, and even daily, Communion (canon 863), and that religious superiors are to promote the same among their subjects (canon 595).

The Holy Eucharist, then, is to be our food. But ordinary food is assimilated by the eater, so as to become part and parcel of his own body; whereas this spiritual food, on the contrary, assimilates us to itself. Our Blessed Lord takes fuller possession of our souls, penetrates and dominates them more completely by His grace, draws us more powerfully to Himself. Thus the more we surrender ourselves to His quickening Life, the more truly we can cry with the Apostle: ''Tis no longer I that live, 'tis Christ liveth in me.' And through Christ, being united with Him, the members of His Mystical Body are united one with another. Their communion or fellowship with each other is in the Body and Blood of the Lord; 'we many are one bread, one body, for we all partake of the one bread' (I Cor. X, 17). And thus we may fulfil in Holy Communion the two great commandments, to love God with our whole heart, in that we love Christ; and to love our neighbour as ourselves, for with our neighbour, too, this sacrament brings us into divinest union — at least with those who like ourselves receive it, for with others we can but desire such fellowship, and pray for it.

THE ABIDING PRESENCE. Christ, as we have seen, must be the centre of our lives; and it is mainly through the Blessed Sacrament that He establishes His reign in our hearts. Our daily work should be one unbroken preparation for His sacramental union with us, one unbroken thanksgiving for His perpetual coming. To Him we should take all our troubles and all our joys and all else that befalls us, with a truly personal love for our Emmanuel, which we must make it our first care ever to increase. It is a very helpful practice to spend every day some time

with Him which we are in no way bound so to
spend; whatever our rules or customs may entail
in the way of visits and prayers before the Blessed
Sacrament, they can never excuse us from the
loving duty of seeking out Jesus for ourselves,
and of telling Him we are there, of course under
the sanction of obedience, yet of our own initiative
and because we like to be with Him.   How
astonishing, that any should ever think they have
'nothing to do', when their tabernacled Lord is
dwelling under the same roof! Let it rather be
our care to make time for Him. We must be at
home with Him. Holy Mother Church surrounds
her Lord with stately liturgy and costly palaces,
and that is an expression of loving reverence;
yet, as we think of Him at that first Eucharist
reclining with His disciples, speaking to them as
friends without ceremony and in their own tongue,
we must bethink us that there is an element of
loving familiarity in the gathering that, if so it
may be, is even more priceless.

SIXTH DAY, CONSIDERATION:

POVERTY.

The final end of a retreat, as of all spiritual
effort, is union with God in supernatural love,
a union furthered and safeguarded by the vows
of religion. These latter, as has already been
explained in the third meditation of the second

day, constitute the state of perfection precisely
because they bind those who take them to embrace
the universal means to this union, and to remove
the universal hindrances thereunto. The vows
have thus already been considered in general as
part of the duties of our state; but it is now
time that we turn to them once more, that by
fulfilling them to the uttermost not only in the
letter but in the spirit, we may prepare ourselves
for that final act of charity which is the close
of the retreat, beyond which human perfection
cannot go. They will be the subject of the next
three considerations.

THE VOW. First, then, as regards the vow
of poverty. This is a somewhat thorny subject
to treat, partly because it is a point on which
the constitutions and laws of the various orders
differ, and partly because theologians are not
agreed upon one or two rather important points.
It will be enough, therefore, to lay down some
general principles, which apply to all. Poverty
may be described as the absence of wealth, that
is, of goods which have a money value. Religious
poverty is the voluntary renunciation of wealth,
confirmed by vow. According to St. Thomas
(II-II, q. 188, a. 7) the hindrances to charity which it
removes are chiefly three, namely, the anxiety,
and also the vainglory, which riches bring with
them; and the love of them, which is increased
by their possession. Poverty, it should be noted,

cannot be absolute and entire. Life itself demands, at the least, food and clothing; and religious life, whether of the apostolic or contemplative kind, demands more than this. Consequently, as St. Thomas says in the same place, 'each religious order will be so much the more perfect as regards poverty, according as it has a poverty better adapted to its end'. Our Lord Himself, we may remember, and His disciples, though they lived on alms, yet kept those alms in a common purse. This diversity of practice, springing from the different ends which the orders have in view, obtains in regard both of collective and individual poverty. Into the large question of collective poverty we need not here enter farther. As regards individual poverty, the most fundamental difference is this: the vow may exclude merely the independent use of anything, or it may render the religious entirely incapable of individual ownership. Not of course that a vow, which is of the nature of a promise, can of itself produce such an incapacity: but in certain cases, usually those of solemn vows, the divine authority of the Church superinduces this incapacity, in accordance with the rule of the order, sanctioned by herself.

An offence may be committed against the vow mainly in two ways. In the first place, according to the more common opinion, there is an obligation under vow to maintain a state of poverty, for example, not to possess superfluities, or to

spend money in a way better suited to a rich
man in the world. Nevertheless all are agreed
that, provided a religious has full and valid leave
from superiors for everything that he does, and
apart from any consideration of scandal or the
like, it is very difficult to reach a mortal sin
precisely through failure to maintain a state of
poverty, and therefore considerations which help
us so to maintain it are often treated of rather
under the virtue than under the vow of poverty.
In the second place, sin may be committed by
the independent disposal of anything. Speaking
generally, a mortal sin is reached when the value
of the article so disposed of would suffice for a
mortal sin of theft. Example of such independent
disposal would be the receiving and keeping of
a sum of money without the superior's knowledge
and consent, or the wilful neglect of goods committed to one's care. As for the sum required for
a mortal sin of theft, according to Fr. Lehmkuhl,
and that before the War, two pounds would be a
sufficient sum, apart from peculiar circumstances;
but the various possibilities cannot be discussed
here. To save the vow, it is enough that the
action should not be altogether independent of
the superior's will; thus, there is no sin against
the vow if it be reasonably certain that he is
content that his leave should not be asked.
Finally, the very fact that almost everything
turns on the will of superiors evidently lays a

great responsibility upon them of maintaining the religious poverty alike of the order and of the individual in all its strictness.

THE VIRTUE. The Angelic Doctor, in proving that voluntary poverty is required for the religious state, reminds us (II-II, q. 186, a. 3) that for the perfection of charity 'one must wholly remove one's affections from worldly things; for Augustine, speaking to God, saith, He loveth Thee less who loveth anything together with Thee, which he doth not love because of Thee.' This removing of the affections from worldly things appears to supply us with a virtue corresponding to the vow of poverty, though some, insisting that the absence of goods is a purely external circumstance, deny that such a virtue exists. Yet we may well assume a virtue which moderates our inclination to wealth, to goods which have a money value. Such a virtue will be a part of temperance, taken in the broad sense. Temperance, taken in the strict theological sense, is the virtue which restrains our inclinations there where they are most alluring, that is, in pleasure of taste and touch; but in the wider sense it may be said to restrain our inclination wherever it is allured contrary to right reason. This restraining virtue, then, will correspond to the vow of poverty. 'The virtue of poverty', says Ferrari [1], 'has a wider

---

[1] Ferrari, *De statu religioso commentarium, ad usum praesertim Clericorum regularium S. Pauli*, p. 158. The above

scope than the vow. The latter binds religious
only; the former, insomuch as it excludes a
disordered inclination to temporal goods, binds
those in the world also. . . . But the perfection
of this virtue lies in this, that, content with what
is strictly necessary, we sincerely embrace a life
that is really poor, after the example of Christ
and of the saints who were religious, and moreover we prefer the lack of superfluities, and what
is poorer in food, clothing, furniture, dwelling
to what is better, and thus join the practice of
poverty to the desire.' This virtue, then, like
that of chastity, which belongs to the virtue of
temperance more directly, is binding upon all;
but to observe either in the most perfect way
a definite external renunciation is required, undertaken by vow under obligation of sin. In the
case of the virtue which we are considering, it
is this external renunciation which is more easily
understood by the word 'poverty'; but we may
well speak of the internal detachment as 'poverty
of spirit', without wishing to assert that it covers
the whole of what is signified by that expression
in the gospel. But whatever difference there may
be in expression or theory, it should be borne
in mind that all are agreed that the practice of
poverty, embracing both perfect dependence and

passage is taken from *Ius Regulare quo regitur Societas Iesu*,
by E. Fine, S. J., p. 391.

also, within the limits of prudence, the absence of superfluities and even of conveniences, is highly meritorious, and a necessary part of a fervent religious life.

THE PRACTICE. It is clear, then, that there are two points to be looked to: in the first place, proper dependence, and in the second place, the poor life. The former evidently consists in having neither more nor less at one's disposal or in one's keeping than the superior intends one to have, to incur neither greater nor less expense than he desires, in a word, to make his will our own in all that concerns our handling of external goods. How far we may go without actual recourse to the superior must be judged from the rules and customs of the order and, within these, from the superior's own wishes, so far as they are clear to us. On the one hand we should endeavour not to increase his burden unduly, nor on the other to carry on as our own lords and masters and leave him in the dark. Again, love of common life is in many points a particular application of the virtue of poverty or detachment, so far as this virtue embraces perfect dependence. It is an offence against the vow, and a great blow struck against religious discipline, if individuals contrive to secure for themselves without proper sanction extra comforts or articles of better quality; contrariwise, it belongs to the practice of the virtue to have a horror of all exceptions that are

not absolutely necessary, and to value all that
belongs to common life, precisely because we
have it in common with all our brethren from
the hands of our superior. Another point that
deserves mention here is the keeping of accounts. Not all are called to be capable finan-
ciers, or indeed to have much to do with
money at all; but what can be demanded from
all is that, whenever they do handle it, they
should keep a clear and accurate account of
what has been received and what has been spent,
in greater or less detail according to the requirements of the case and the wishes of those
in authority.

As regards the poor life, we have seen that
it would be wrong to assume that the greater
the external want, the more perfect the practice
of the virtue. The first and chief criterion is
the work which it is our duty to perform. But
the virtue of poverty will evidently demand that
we should rid ourselves of a superfluity. Who
could enumerate all a religious' possible superfluities, in toilet and clothing, in books and
stationery, indeed, in sheer ornamentation or
amusement? These are the idols of religious
life; they are the trifles which those who have
made a great renunciation try to sneak back
from the holocaust. One good safeguard is the
scrutinium paupertatis, an occasional scrutiny
of our cell, to see if we can discover therein

anything superfluous or worldly, and much more, of course, anything for which we have not proper leave. We may also consider how we have treated what has been at our disposal, whether in or out of our cell, and whether we have been wasteful, untidy, extravagant. It is easy to offend in the matter of books; something has been said about them in the consideration for the fifth day. Cleanliness, again, both in one's own person and in all else, is not opposed to poverty, but a part of it. It indicates a proper sense of stewardship, which means a better care of what is entrusted to us; there are of course other reasons also, such as the care that our ministry, where we have any relations with outsiders, should be without offence.

But a proper regard for poverty should also manifest itself directly in the religious' intercourse with the world outside. It ill becomes him to show himself over-eager for money, and all that money can buy. 'Freely you have received, freely give', says Our Blessed Lord (Matt. x, 8). It is scarcely possible amid the financial stress of our time to carry out such a precept literally on anything like a large scale; nevertheless we should be trying how much we can give for how little, rather than the reverse. The work of the ministry, the work of teaching and the like, are not to be measured against an earthly price or reward; and it may produce a painful impression if there be an excessive or too importunate demand for money. Much more, of course, will this be the case if a religious be observed to crave for what has no relation to his spiritual work at all, but is mere luxury, such as choice food or various amusements and personal comforts. Rather let us beware of being too much at home with the rich and their way of life; it is the poor of Christ who have the first claim to our heart, and to be at home with them is of itself some guarantee of a true spirit of poverty.

Poverty is the bulwark of religious life, and as such as we must love and cherish it, after the example of Him who, whereas He was rich, became poor for our sakes.

SIXTH DAY, THIRD MEDITATION:

THE SACRED HEART.

Just as in the preceding meditation we have devoted ourselves to the Holy Eucharist in itself, without attempting to follow the historical sequence of events at the Last Supper, so here we may devote ourselves entirely to the thought of the Sacred Heart of Jesus, without necessarily endeavouring to follow the events that follow upon the Last Supper. It is indeed to the Sacred Heart that our thoughts naturally turn when we behold Jesus prostrate in His agony, unfaltering in His loving purpose to redeem the world, yet, to use the words of the gospels, grieved, distressed, dismayed at the price to be paid, and (must we not add, if we are to explain the paroxysm of that woe?) at the scant fruit of it all. If the key-note of the devotion to the Sacred Heart is unrequited love, it is no less that of the agony.

THE APPEAL. In order to have a thorough understanding of this devotion, it is best to approach it on its dogmatic side. We adore the Sacred Humanity of Christ, consisting of His Soul and His Body, with divine adoration, because it is the Sacred Humanity of the Second Person of the Blessed Trinity, of Him who is God. We do not adore the Humanity as something apart from the Person whose Humanity it is, but we adore the Person *in* the Humanity. And in the same way we adore any part of that Humanity, once more not as apart and by itself, but with reference to the Person whose it is, whom we adore in it. And so it is, for example, with a king whose hand we might kiss; our act of veneration and submission would not be addressed to the hand taken by itself, but to the person to whom the hand belonged. In this way, therefore, we adore the Sacred Heart of Our Lord, not as considered in itself, as it were, and apart from Him, but as the very Heart of the God-man, of Him who is the Second

Person of the Blessed Trinity. That is the true and ancient doctrine of the Incarnation, as much exemplified in our forefathers' devotion to the Five Wounds or in the devotion to the Sacred Face as in that which we are now making our peculiar study.

But next, we look for some reason for the selection of the particular part of Christ's Body to which our adoration is to be paid, at all events if the adoration of that part is to constitute a strong and permanent devotion in the Church. Even as in a king we venerate the hand as the symbol of power or authority, so in the case of Our Blessed Lord there can be nothing arbitrary in the choice made by the Church of the peculiar object of her devotion, and still less in a choice made by Our Blessed Lord Himself. The Sacred Heart of Our Lord is here taken, as the heart is often taken in ordinary usage, as the seat of the emotions. The heart is easily affected by strong emotion, and is used to symbolise it. And if we ask what is the precise emotion which we are to represent Our Blessed Lord to ourselves as undergoing, there can be no doubt as to the answer; it is unrequited love. 'Behold', He said to St. Margaret Mary, 'Behold this Heart which has so loved men, that it has spared nothing, even to exhausting and consuming itself, to testify to them its love; and by way of gratitude I receive from the greater number only ingratitude, in their irreverences and sacrileges, and in the coldness and contempt which they have for Me in this sacrament of love. But what hurts Me most is this, that it is hearts which are consecrated to Me that behave thus.' These words are to be found both in the autobiography which St. Margaret Mary wrote by obedience, and in the first life of her, written immediately upon her death by two of her former novices, in whose arms she had died (cf. *Vie et œuvres de la B. Marguerite - Marie Alacoque*, edited by Mgr. Gauthey, Archbishop of Besançon: vol. II, p. 102, and vol. I, p. 137). We find here that it is especially of the coldness and contempt displayed towards Him in His Eucharistic presence that Our Lord complains, and yet again, it is more especially of such behaviour on the part of those consecrated to Him. The nearer they should be to Him, the more He feels their neglect. Not that it can cause Him true suffering now, if we wish to be theologically exact; but it has caused Him bitter suffering once — most of all, we may well think, during the agony in the garden; and His feelings are still the same, though without the suffering. To speak and think of Him as still yearning, as still disappointed, and so forth, is the nearest approach we can make to realising the tremendous truth, though we must beware of holding any positive error.

OUR ANSWER. After the great revelation of
His Sacred Heart to which we have just referred,
Our Lord asked for the institution of the feast
of the Sacred Heart, such as we know it today,
as a reparation of honour for the indignities received by the Sacred Heart while exposed upon
our altars in the Blessed Sacrament. What we
are asked to do is to honour the Sacred Heart
of our Divine Saviour, and to honour it in reparation for others' neglect and contempt, and this
again more especially as manifested towards Our
Blessed Lord in His Real Presence upon our altars,
and yet again, more especially as manifested towards Him by those consecrated to His service.
How can we resist such an appeal? On the one
side we have Our Blessed Lord awaiting eagerly
some attention, some devotion, in answer to the
prodigies of His love; on the other side we have
mankind, so many knowing Him not, so many
who know Him denying His presence among
us, so many who confess His presence ignoring
it.   And yet it is not of all these that He
complains most, but of ourselves, that we
make little or nothing of the priceless privilege
we enjoy, of having our Emmanuel under the
same roof as ourselves. We must atone, then,
for our neglect, we must be generous, not
serving in a dogged or stoic spirit, but out of
love; we must no longer ask ourselves what
we are obliged to do, how little we can do, but

rather how much we can do, whether we could not do a thousand times more than we have done hitherto. Ours must be the spirit of glad sacrifice; to lack either the sacrifice or the gladness is the sign of a lukewarm soul. Above all, we must live that Eucharistic life of which we spoke in the last meditation; no doubt our moments of greater fervour and greater love will be when Jesus comes into our breast, but we must be with Him at other times also when we can, and even when we must away we must still leave our hearts glued to His. Our joys and sorrows, our hopes and fears, all our life must be His, and whatever is not Himself must be burnt up and destroyed in the furnace of His Heart.

THE FIRST FRIDAY. The consecration of the first Friday of the month is now so firmly rooted in the Church, that it needs no words to commend it. It was demanded by Our Lord through St. Margaret Mary, and we may say that His demand has been complied with. Yet not so fully as He, and therefore we, could wish; and we need to do all in our power to renew once a month on this day our devotion to the Sacred Heart, and to help others to do the same. And so, in reflecting upon this, we are inevitably brought to the question of the Nine Fridays, a question which can hardly be passed over in silence in a con-

sideration such as this. The view here to be
set forth has been advocated by several Catholic writers; but it has not found universal acceptance, and there are also not a few who,
while zealous for First Friday Communions, do
not consider it prudent to press the devotion
of the Nine Fridays in particular. Such, indeed,
appears to have been the mind of the first pro-
moters of the devotion at a time when even in
its essentials it was far from finding universal
acceptance. What is here written, however, has
not been written with any controversial purpose;
at least all can agree in promoting the First
Friday devotion in general, and in hoping for
a rich reward.

The promise itself is reported in a letter
written by St. Margaret Mary to the Mère de
Saumaise, her former superior, in 1688: 'One
Friday, during Holy Communion, He said these
words to His unworthy slave, if she be not deceived: "I promise thee, in the exceeding mercy
of My Heart, that the all-powerful love thereof
will grant to all those who shall communicate
on nine first Fridays of the month in succession
the grace of final repentance; they shall not die
in My displeasure and without receiving their
sacraments, but My Divine Heart will make itself their assured refuge at their last moment."
(Gauthey, vol. II, pp. 397—398). This same promise is quoted from this same letter in the first

life of St. Margaret Mary, already referred to, with only the slightest verbal changes. With regard to the precise form of words in which the promise is couched, two points should be noted. In the first place, the use of the phrase, 'if she be not deceived', does not imply any doubt in the mind of the writer as to the reality of the revelation and the promise; such expressions were inserted in obedience to her superior, the Mère Greyfié, a fact vouched for by the Mère Greyfié herself in her memoir of St. Margaret Mary (Gauthey, vol. I, pp. 175, 361). Secondly, the phrase 'without receiving their sacraments' is not a usual one in French; it must not be understood to mean that all who perform the nine Fridays will have the last sacraments at their death, but must be understood from the context. What is primarily promised is the grace of final repentance, the grace of not dying under Our Lord's displeasure; and it appears right to understand 'their sacraments' as the sacraments by which this end is to be assured. 'In the hour of death one may be either in a state of grace, or in need of becoming so. No one can enter into that state without desiring the Sacrament of Penance, and the actual reception either of that sacrament, of Extreme Unction, or even of the Eucharist may for many be a necessity' (*The Great Promise*, by Fr. A. Vermeersch, S. J., p. 12).

14 *

Some, more or less alarmed at the greatness of the promise, prefer to make it in some way conditional; but there is no warrant for this in the words themselves, nor does there appear to be any solid theological reason for refusing to accept them at the face value. The Council of Trent, whence the chief difficulty is usually drawn, only condemns the Lutheran doctrine that the *act of faith* can have for its proper object the individual's own state of grace or predestination, and does not exclude a moral certainty which evidently falls short of this. We can feel reasonably sure that the promise was made, perhaps even that this is the right interpretation of it; but such assurance falls far short of the absolute infallibility of faith. Still, it does much to comfort timid souls, and to enkindle the lukewarm, and experience shows that the long sustained effort leads to great and lasting good. Almighty God can, if He please, so provide that none who make the nine Fridays shall die impenitent, just as the man will never be born that will sin against the Holy Ghost and truly repent (cf. Mark III, 29, with note in Westminster Version). This is not to invent new sacraments or make any other such change in the economy of grace, but merely to tell us beforehand some of the results, for our own profit.

In conclusion, attention may be called to the movement for the consecration of families to the Sacred Heart, a movement evidently entirely in the spirit of the revelations and promises made to St. Margaret Mary, and much encouraged by the Holy See. Religious, while promoting it as best they can, may well show the way by consecrating their own houses to the same Divine Heart.

———

SEVENTH DAY.

THE PASSION.

PATRON: Our Lord, under the invocation of the Sacred Heart.

READING: Mark XV; Philip. I, 21—II, 18; Imitation II, 11—12.

FIRST MEDITATION: The Jews (The Agony, Annas, Caiphas).

SECOND MEDITATION: Pilate (The First Encounter, Herod, Pilate's later devices).

CONSIDERATION: Chastity (Temptation, Personal Precautions, The Precautions of Religious Life).

THIRD MEDITATION: Resolutions: generosity (The Three Classes of Men, The Three Kinds of Humility, Resolutions).

✠

THY SACRED HEART.

Teach all, O Lord,
The treasures of Thy love,
    Thy Sacred Heart,
    And all Thou art,
Thy life, Thy death, Thy reign above.

Teach those, O Lord,
Who live within Thy fold,
    To love yet more
    Whom they adore,
Atoning where the world is cold.

Yea, more, O Lord,
Souls vowed for aye to Thee
    Thou grievest to find
    Heedless and blind;
Teach us what Thou wouldst have us be!

Teach us, O Lord,
Save with Thee to have no part;
    Set us on fire
    With one desire,
To live and die within Thy Heart!

———

SEVENTH DAY, FIRST MEDITATION:
THE JEWS.

WE may now begin to turn more directly to the facts of the Passion. The Holy Eucharist plays so large a part in the Last Supper, that having meditated upon the former we need not come back upon the latter. But it may profit us to reflect upon the Agony of the Garden, taken in itself, and to make this the beginning of our thoughts on the Passion. In this meditation therefore we take up the story from the end of the Last Supper, and carry it on to the time when Our Lord is brought before Pilate. During this time the Jewish authorities are moving on their own initiative; afterwards they are in the main endeavouring to influence Pilate. The story may be conveniently divided into three parts. The first covers the time during which Our Lord is still a free man; the second two mark stages in the Jewish proceedings against Him.

THE AGONY. After Jesus had entered the garden of Gethsemane, He left all but three of the apostles behind, and immediately the deep emotion which possessed Him began to manifest itself more visibly. He left even the three, and went a little way forward, and then it had full play. Dismay, alarm, disappointment, grief, all these are present to Him; present to Him, it is true, because He permits them, and yet the natural outcome of that vivid realization of past, present and future, to which He now abandoned Himself, as natural as our own emotions are to us. We may consider a few of the thoughts that filled His mind. There was the thought of the physical sufferings that He was to endure, and of outrages and insults. The pain of anticipation is often harder to bear than the reality, and in the case of Christ there was nothing wanting to the vividness of the picture, or to the certainty that it was indeed to be. He cried aloud, to express the utter shrinking of His human nature, but in perfect subordination the while to the will of His Father. Again, the sins of the whole world and of all time were upon Him. As St. Paul puts it, Him who knew not sin God had made sin in our behalf (II Cor. V, 21). That mysterious identification of Himself with sin, that vicarious guilt, was for Him a thing very real, and shame and horror at the loathed contamination overcame Him. Men look for some sensation in their daily paper; some crime more ghastly than usual pleases the editor with the prospect of a better sale, and the jaded reader with a new thrill. Of the grave offence against God they reck little or nothing; but to Christ it was everything. He saw the daily record of sin, published and unpublished, and He saw to how little purpose for many would be the shedding of His Blood. His agony was unspeakable; and

an angel came to comfort Him, to show Him,
it may be, all the loyalty and utter devotion
that was to be offered Him through the course
of the world, by all His faithful, and by those
more especially consecrated to His service. If
we have added to His agony, we must also
add to His consolation. One other little thought
we may take away with us, for the benefit of
our meditation. Christ, we are told, because of
all this agony, prayed the more earnestly and
intensely; a lesson to us that the difficulty of
prayer is something to overcome, and not matter
for despondency or sluggishness. Christ found
the apostles asleep; that meant not only more
sorrow and disappointment for Him, but less
grace for them in their need. 'Sleep ye now
and take your rest!' They had taken their rest
at an ill time; better for them had they slept
through all that followed, rather than have shown
such cowardice!

ANNAS. The inward agony is now over, and
for the rest of the Passion, through all the intensity of suffering, we see no flinching, nor indeed any sign of internal commotion, save possibly that cry on the Cross: 'My God, my God,
why hast Thou forsaken me?' First of all there
is Judas to be faced, the traitor with his kiss.
It is Judas' last chance, as Christ murmurs to
him words which show how He understands all
too well the fallen apostle's purpose, and which

invite him to repent. Judas is perhaps flurried, but he is hardened. Nor would any change on his part make any difference now, so far as Christ is concerned; the betrayal is complete, and he is needed no more. Only, had he hearkened to those words of the Master, he might yet have turned to hope and penitent love, and have emulated the tears of Peter.

And now Christ faces the men that have come out to seize Him. Roman soldiers are there in orderly array, part of the cohort that garrisoned Jerusalem, lent by Pilate to the high-priests: now they are quiet enough, but later they will have their own cruel sport with Christ. The Jews were exempt from conscription, so that the cohort would be recruited from other Palestinians and foreigners, no friends to the Jews, and with nothing of the Roman character. Besides these soldiers there is a mob with knives and cudgels, including, no doubt, a body of the Temple police and servants of the high-priest, and private individuals brought hither by various motives. 'I am he!' The words rang out, and their divine power was at once felt. In Greek, which language Our Lord may well have been using with this mixed mob, the two words are the same as those of the Divine Name, 'I am'; and Our Lord intended the twofold meaning — not merely to tell them He was the one for whom they were looking, but to assert His Divine power at this supreme moment of yielding Himself into their hands. Their falling to the ground, therefore, was the result of His pronouncing with intended power His own Divine Name. 'Put back thy sword into its place!' If He chose to exert power, He stood in no need of human weapons. Peter did a bold deed in the excitement of the moment; but he lacked moral courage, that unflinching endurance of the dislike and scorn of fellow-creatures which is so much harder to face than bullet or bayonet. And the other apostles were less bold even than Peter, and so avoided the danger into which his love drew him. 'This is your hour!' Christ is led away to Annas.

The Romans, like Herod before them, had no scruple in deposing high-priests and appointing new ones. Annas was one of those deposed, but he still held a position of great influence, as is shown by the fact that five of his sons and Caiphas his son-in-law held the office after him. Doubtless he was regarded by many as the true high-priest *de iure*. He appears to have been avaricious, arrant, unscrupulous, and he and his house were feared and hated by the Pharisees and people. Perhaps he was the real mover in the proceedings against Our Lord, and there can have been no legal justification for the examination to which he now subjected Him. It was a barefaced attempt to see how his victim's

death could best be encompassed. Christ would
not seem to lend Himself in any way to such
an outrage upon divine and human law, and
when one of the attendants struck him with hand
or rod He bore it meekly, but did not withdraw
from His position. If evidence was sought as to
the true facts, there were plenty who could give
it, and in proper process of law.

CAIPHAS. The trial before the Sanhedrin seems
to have opened as soon as possible; it must have
been getting very late, for it was night (John
XIII, 30) when Judas left the supper-room. There
is nothing to show that the night-sitting was in
itself illegal; the Sadducean families that supplied the high-priests and dominated Jewish affairs paid no heed to the regulations of the
Pharisees, which moreover probably date from
a time when there could be no question of putting them into practice. False witnesses were
sought against Christ, but apparently the necessity of preparing and priming them had been
overlooked, and it needed no words on Our
Lord's part to show that they were inconsistent
with each other. A special attempt seems to
have been made to prove that Our Lord said
that He would destroy the Temple, but here
too a want of proper rehearsal resulted in a
break-down. Evidently the Jewish authorities had
been so taken up with the question how to get
Christ into their power that they had not con-

certed measures for dealing with Him when they
got Him. Caiphas challenged Our Lord to defend Himself, but He was silent — it was already obvious that there was no case. It was
apparently as though to compel Him to speak
that Caiphas as high priest put the supreme
question, adjuring Him to tell them whether He
were the Christ the Son of God. As we gather
from St. Luke, it was Our Lord's solemn reference to Daniel that brought Him questions
from all sides, 'Art thou, then, the Son of God?'
He had not refused to answer the high-priest's
direct and official question, nor did He refuse
an answer now on so vital a question to the
leaders of His nation. They counted it blasphemy. Blasphemy it would have been in any
ordinary man, but the one tremendous question
which they would not ask themselves was, whether
in His case it might not be the simple truth.

And now we turn to Peter awhile, so ardent
and yet so cowardly in his love. The courtyard
of Annas seems to have been also that of Caiphas.
We may suppose that the first denial was to the
portress while Christ was still before Annas, that
the second denial, or group of denials, when
Christ had left Annas, and that the third was
made towards the end of the trial. The vehe-
mence of his denial increased with the persistence
of his accusers, until in answer to their alleging
his very speech he began to curse and to swear.

And Jesus, who was probably at the moment being led away from before the Sanhedrin, 'looked on Peter'. And Peter remembered, and understood that the now suffering Master had not changed towards him, and that he himself was Peter still — the same as of yore, save only for an ocean of tears and sorrow that must find speedy outlet. We leave him weeping. The Divine Victim Himself had been struck and mocked after His trial, and how long these outrages were continued, and whether He was allowed some rest in the night, we are not told. Judas is yielding to utter despair; most fatal sin of all, he has come to disbelieve that God is ready to forgive.

SEVENTH DAY, SECOND MEDITATION:
PILATE.

The Passion and Death of Our Saviour is God's answer to the sins of the world, and we are right in confronting it with all that is most grievous in the history of human wrong-doing. He knew all the crimes of mankind, and took them upon Himself. But we must also make the Passion a personal matter for ourselves, and apply all its tremendous power to the emendation of the past year, and in particular to the keeping of our resolution. By the mercy of God it may well be that the faults against which we most need to guard are not in themselves very serious; but we must pray for light and grace to make much even of small things, in the true spirit of religious life. Judas was unfaithful because he misapplied the common fund to his own purposes; the religious who uses money for his own comforts and advantages to a degree beyond what is intended by superiors, is walking the way of Judas, even if he has not progressed far therein. Pilate committed an awful crime through irresolution and human respect; and how often a religious may fail through lack of moral courage! Thus the great lessons of the Passion must be applied to our daily lives, if they are to bear solid fruit. The Passion does not merely tell us to avoid hell or mortal sin; it stirs us up to war upon our least faults, to utter crucifixion of self with Christ, to perfect love.

THE FIRST ENCOUNTER. We left Our Lord being guarded for the night; how many hours He was thus, and whether it meant rest or torment, we do not know. But it was still very early in the morning when the chief priests and the elders and the scribes met once more, and debated how to secure His execution. In their own tribunal they had condemned Him to death, but the power of capital punishment had been taken from them, perhaps only lately, and the question was, how to get Pilate to ratify their sentence. To judge from the account of their discussion with Pilate in St. John's Gospel (John XVIII, 29—31), they hoped to do this without any Roman trial at all. In this they appear to have eventually succeeded, but only with immense difficulty. Pilate soon persuaded himself of Jesus' innocence, and almost from the first sought to release Him. He must have had some knowledge of what was passing in Jerusalem and Palestine, and in any case he knew that it needed something more than zeal for Roman supremacy to bring all the chiefs of the nation in vehement accusation before him. They had been compelled to think of some capital charge that would go down with him, and sedition was the obvious one. Pilate, however, was not taken in; it was jealousy that had brought them, jealousy of a religious teacher that was not of their set or of their ways.

But the Sanhedrists had foreseen that it might be necessary to resort to browbeating. Their arguments were not worth much, but Pilate hesitated to offend them mortally by an open repulse, because they might make matters uncomfortable for him here, and still more at Rome. And he thought he had found a loop-hole; he discovered that Christ was a Galilaean, and decided to refer the whole matter to Herod. As likely as not it was a question of jurisdiction that had made them enemies, in which case Pilate's action would be especially pleasing to

Herod. But Our Lord did not gratify Herod's pride as Pilate did; nor was the latter quit of his trouble.

HEROD. Herod expected to be vastly entertained; he thought that the wonder-worker from Galilee would be only too willing to show off his tricks before him, and he himself in return would be gracious, and perhaps do something to help him. His trifling was little to the liking of the chief priests and scribes; what they wanted was Christ's death, and they stood by vehemently accusing Him, careless of degradation and contempt if they might secure their end. But Christ would have nothing to do with Herod's trifling either; was it the figure of His great Forerunner that He kept before His mind, slain to please a dancing girl? For a moment Herod was aghast; then he saw how to save his face. He shrugged his shoulders. 'The man's a fool!' And so he set him at naught; but in that very mockery there was the malignity of piqued vanity. There was still no answer. Herod scorned Christ; but Christ's scorn for Herod was deeper still. It was in keeping with his treatment of Christ that Herod should say that He had done nothing to deserve death: He was more fool than knave!

Herod is the type of frivolity, of those who are blown like straws upon the surface of things, and have become incapable of appreciating the deeper issues of life. This surface-existence and

15 *

lack of serious thinking is one of the characteristic evils of our own time, and is nourished
by a devotion to sensational dailies and other
cheap literature; also upon irreverence, as to
which something was said at the outset of the
retreat. Besides cultivating reverence, and im-
pressing upon ourselves the great truths of our
faith through meditation, it will be of service
to cultivate worthier and more serious tastes
even in matters not directly spiritual. Through
frivolity one may come to treat those who would
really be of spiritual profit with some touch of
the spirit in which Herod treated Christ.

PILATE'S LATER DEVICES. It was a blow to
Pilate to see Jesus return. He protested that
the prisoner was innocent, but proposed to chastise Him all the same before releasing Him —
a proposal weak as it was wicked, which let the
Sanhedrists see that they were gaining ground.
Pilate was perhaps already alarmed at the gathering crowds, when he remembered the reason
why they had come, the annual custom of releasing the prisoner for whom they should ask.
He appears to have arbitrarily limited their choice
in order to secure his own purpose of having
Jesus released, for there seems no reason why
they should not have asked for one of the two
thieves afterwards crucified with Him. But the
chief priests and scribes succeeded, perhaps with
some difficulty, in moving the multitude to de-

mand Barabbas. For the latter it was a release
utterly unhoped for; but Christ was reputed with
the wicked, that for His sake we should be prepared to suffer gladly the loss of reputation and
good name, should His service so demand it,
and in so far as it would entail no fault on our
part or our neighbour's.

Meanwhile Pilate, foiled once more, has re-
verted to his earlier plan: 'I will chastise him
and let him go.' Apparently he ordered the
scourging, not as the usual preliminary to crucifixion, but in place of it, hoping thus to satisfy
the Sanhedrists; and for this reason it would
be likely to be a scourging of exceptional severity. When the final sentence of crucifixion
actually came, the scourging had already been
inflicted, and there was no question of repeating
it. The scourges used would probably have a
wooden handle, with two or three long lashes
of hide; into these, pieces of bone or metal were
sometimes fastened, but we cannot tell for certain
whether this was so in the case of Our Lord.
The victim would be tied to a low pillar, and
the stripes would be inflicted by trained hands
with tremendous force upon his bare back. It
is usual and natural to think of this terrible
torture inflicted upon Our Lord's innocent flesh
as an atonement for men's indulgence of their
flesh, for impurity and sensuality of every kind.
And the crowning of thorns which followed may

well have been intended by Divine Providence
as the punishment of our pride. It was an or-
ganised game, in which practically the whole
cohort, comprising several hundred men, joined
in. This cohort appears to have constituted the
regular garrison of the tower Antonia, to the
north of the Temple area. The soldiers stripped
Christ, and then put about Him one of their
own scarlet cloaks, in derision of his kingly claim;
their own cloaks were part of their military uniform, but the recognised royal mantle was very
similar. Then they plaited and put on His head
a crown of long, sharp thorns, such as grow pro-
fusely in the neighbourhood, and may have been
lying about for the making of fires. Soldier after
soldier advanced and knelt before Him in homage
— 'Hail, King of the Jews!' — and then rose and
spat on Him, and took His reed-sceptre from His
bound bands and struck His head with it, upon
the crown of thorns.

After all this Pilate again led Him out —
'Behold the man!' Shepherds and kings had
beheld Him and adored; Pilate and the Jews
beheld Him only to do Him to death. In what
a dreadful condition He must have been! Yet
the blood-lust is now on the multitude, and the
Sanhedrists are still exciting them. Even now
there is something about Christ that moves Pilate to awe and reverence, and the mention of
a claim to Divine Sonship alarms him into further

questions. Even this last chance is lost when he is threatened with complaints to Caesar. And the Jews! They have said they have no king but Caesar, that Christ's blood is to be upon them and upon their children! 'He came unto His own, and His own received Him not.' But to the Gentiles the portals of salvation are to be flung open wide, to such as believe in Christ and bear their cross after Him. We hear the sentence, passed without real trial and due to fear and weakness; it is our condemnation that is upon Him, and with Him we hope to pass through Passion and Cross to a glorious Resurrection.

SEVENTH DAY, CONSIDERATION:

CHASTITY.

No words need here be spent in praise of chastity. Absolute virginity is plainly recommended as the more perfect way both by Our Lord and St. Paul, and has always been so recognised by the Church. Priestly celibacy is a matter of Church discipline, and it falls outside our scope to discuss it; but in the religious state the vow of chastity is an essential. The religious binds himself not to marry, and to eschew all that in his unmarried state would be a sin against holy purity. The offence against the vow is measured by the offence against the virtue. To

a mortal sin of impurity is added a mortal sin
of sacrilege. A sin against purity can only be
venial either because it is not fully deliberate,
or because the pleasure indulged in is not of
a strictly venereal or lustful kind, even though
it is 'sensual'; under these circumstances the sin
against the vow is also merely venial. Pleasure
to the senses may of course be lawful, if done
with a good motive; the City clerk on his holidays, for example, may enjoy the comfort of
being in flannels, and so of other sensations.
It is such pleasure as this that we have called
above 'sensual', though not strictly venereal. Evidently, however, the exact line of demarcation
will not always be easy to draw, especially in
the case of the sense of touch, wherein pleasure
most easily runs into what is forbidden, at all
events where there is question of touching human beings. In general, sin may be committed
either by desiring a sinful act, or by taking
pleasure in the thought of it; also, of course,
by running into dangerous occasions, whether in
respect of thought, word or deed.

TEMPTATION. The mere fact of his vocation
does not exempt the religious from the ordinary
temptations of mankind, but only guarantees him
special helps to victory, provided he himself
tries to be faithful. The second vow is in itself
a very difficult one for flesh and blood; matrimony was intended partly as a remedy for con-

cupiscence, and speaking generally, they who contemn it expose themselves to greater danger thereby. It is only the abundant grace of God that can make the victory easy; it is folly to rely upon ourselves, but we must humbly and earnestly implore His aid, and confidently too, since it is His call that has put us into a position of such peculiar and especial dependence upon His grace. And we must endeavour to do all that lies in ourselves, not merely by the cooperation of our will, but also by informing ourselves as to the best means to cope with temptation.

Whether in the case of a temptation to desire or to mere pleasure it must be remembered that it is resistance to the temptation that matters, not the cessation of it. The latter does not always depend on us, nor is it necessarily better for us, since we may be meriting greatly. Temptations, it has been said, are the raw material of glory. We must avoid worry. When we find ourselves tempted, the best thing to do is to offer a short prayer not merely for ourselves, but even more for others in a like case, and then to make a resolute effort to occupy our minds and even, when it can easily be done, our bodies with other things of a kind that interests us. When the temptation is over, we must not revive it by attempting a searching enquiry as to degree of guilt in the matter. We need not

advert to it again till our next examination of
conscience, and then only shortly. If we think
that we were not prompt enough in rejecting
the temptation, that we dallied with it somewhat, we may mention what we think in our
next confession. Such slovenliness would be venial
sin, the consent of the will not being as yet full;
want of complete consciousness also as a general
rule precludes mortal sin. Indeed, until our conscience is to some extent awakened, there is no
sin at all; without any fault of our own we may
catch ourselves thinking thoughts which in themselves would be sinful, but are not so for us,
because we have not yet adverted to them. It
should be added, however, that a zealous care
for purity makes one in time less liable to such
unpleasant surprises. In all cases where we think
it not unlikely that there was sin, we may explain in confession what after a brief and calm
review appears to us to represent the facts; it
is dangerous to attempt to put such phenomena
under the microscope. We must be content with
humble trust in our Heavenly Father, without
seeking for more light than He gives us. For the
consolation of timorous souls, however, it may
be pointed out how unlikely it is that they have
given way to sin, when the mere possibility of
having done so fills them at all times with horror.

PERSONAL PRECAUTIONS. What is of supreme
importance is the prompt and resolute turning aside

from such thoughts to others that are lawful and
not dangerous. Not that in the thought itself, the
mere mental picture as such, apart from any
pleasure in it or desire to realise it, there is of absolute necessity sin; doctors and priests, to speak
of no others, may have at times to turn their attention to very unsavoury topics. Yet sin is to be
found not merely in direct wish or pleasure, but
also in consent to dangerous occasions which are
really unnecessary and can be avoided without
great trouble. Where a true necessity exists, God
will give His help; where it does not, the sin varies
according to the degree of the danger. It stands
to reason that we should not without necessity
allow thoughts to remain in our minds which in
themselves are alluring, and with an allurement
that means mortal sin if it prevails. An occasion
such as that is in the last degree dangerous.
But then there are also thoughts which are on
the border-line, and thoughts which are obviously
concerned rather with matters 'sensual', in the
sense in which we have used the word above,
than with anything strictly venereal. Evidently
the danger from these may be greater or less;
nevertheless a proper zeal and love for the second
vow eschews them all, except in so far as there is
real necessity. In this connection it is sometimes
useful to apply St. Ignatius' test, to consider
whether the beginning, middle and end of a train
of thought be all wholly good; sometimes it may

be found that a train of thought which seems
specious in its beginning invariably ends, or is
apt to end, in the flesh. That is a sign whence
it comes.

In the matter of conversation the same caution
must evidently be exercised as in thought, and
all the more so because others would be involved
in the sin. The fascination of forbidden print
is the fascination of sin, even though the full
guilt of mortal sin be not there. Language that
is in any measure or in any sense dirty becomes
a religious as little as mud upon his habit. There
is sometimes a danger that it may seem a grand
thing to display knowledge on things sexual,
and to dispense questionable stories to admiring
innocents. The harm done may be enormous;
religious who had hitherto made much of the
holy virtue, whose life had been as the angels',
may come to fill their minds with unwholesome
and noxious matter, and their conversation will
in turn become tainted. Anything like 'soft'
conversation is also a danger. *Saepe videtur esse
caritas et est magis carnalitas,* says A Kempis
(I, 15, 2); there may be more of the flesh in our
affection than we suppose. Talk of this kind is
a sufficient proof of it, and also a continual
seeking for the company of some of our brethren,
to the avoidance of others.

What has just been said on the subject of
conversation, however, must not be taken to imply

that all knowledge of such subjects is evil and to be avoided. On the contrary, in these dangers the absence of such knowledge may itself be the cause of temptation and difficulty, not merely to religious themselves, but to children leaving their care. It appears to be widely held among those competent to form an opinion that these latter need nowadays to be sufficiently instructed in sexual questions; the difficulty seems rather to centre on the question as to how this is best done. Some would have it done privately: others, as has been said (p. 168), would have it led up to gradually and easily through botany and biology: others would have it insinuated insensibly, while the children are being taught to honour Our Lady by reason of her special privileges. All these ways seem good, and perhaps they can all be practised at once; in any case the problem is one that has to be faced, and in time experience will doubtless show more clearly what is the best method.

External behaviour must also be looked to, and the danger from all our senses, especially from our eyes and from the sense of touch. As regards the latter, the best precaution is not to touch another at all, although to do so is not, of course, necessarily or even usually sinful. As regards the eyes, one may lay it down as a general rule that it is not the first look that does the damage, but the second, the return to the

spectacle, perhaps even to gloat over it. In thes
days we cannot hope not to see suggestive pi
tures and the like — public opinion, to say th
least, is not squeamish in the matter — but w
can save ourselves from lingering on them.

THE PRECAUTIONS OF RELIGIOUS LIFE. Muc
in religious life is obviously founded on the a
sumption that the second vow is to be highl
esteemed and carefully guarded, and those wh
fervently accept this view will also fervently accep
its implications. Ample safeguards to chastit
are enforced or encouraged: the regulation of o
intercourse with others, the various kinds of mort
fication, devotion to Our Blessed Lady and t
certain saints more especially eminent for th
virtue, reverence to all as to Christ. We nee
only speak here of the first of these. Hol
Mother Church prescribes the religious enclosure
which is fenced about with ecclesiastical penaltie
and restricts those who are within from passin
out without particular or general leave, or withou
a companion, and further wholly excludes thos
of the opposite sex from passing within. Th
practical working of this law is the business o
superiors, and naturally depends to some exter
upon the nature and work of the order, and th
conditions of time and place. But its spirit i
plain. It is a spirit of recollection and peace. Th
more active a religious is in the world outside
holy and apostolic as his activity may be, th

more need he has of a sure retreat, where his soul may draw fresh strength from undisturbed contemplation of the divine. *Cella continuata dulcescit,* says A Kempis (I, 20, 5) — to learn the sweetness of our cell we must dwell much in it. In the same chapter he lays it down that no one can safely appear before the world save he who would gladly remain unknown, no one can safely speak, save he who would gladly remain silent. To have one's eye open for every sight and one's ear for every gossip is not religious life, and will sooner or later mean danger to the second vow. Again, a companion is a protection against disagreeable incidents of many kinds. Instances have not been wanting of trickery on the part of the ill-disposed, and in these days of glaring publicity a single false step may assume almost international importance. The obstacles to having a companion are not always so serious as they are imagined. Man, after all, is a sociable animal, and is not necessarily startled to find that religious have preserved this instinct.

SEVENTH DAY, THIRD MEDITATION:

RESOLUTIONS, GENEROSITY.

In the consideration for the second day something was said as to the matter and manner of retreat resolutions, that is, as to the ways of

discovering what is the right resolution to take
and to the form according to which it woul
be well to draw it up. But now, when w
should no longer delay to put our resolutio
or resolutions into final shape, it is not s
much more light that we must seek as res
lution to use to the full the light which w
possess. Or, to put it another way, it is tim
to look to practice rather than to gather inform
ation. And yet every serious attempt to men
our conduct increases to some extent the ligh
which guides us.

THE THREE CLASSES OF MEN. The questio
then, is this: are we in earnest? Do we mea
business? St. Ignatius realises how all-importan
it is that, if we may so speak, we should b
brought up to scratch, and it is for this purpos
that he proposes the consideration of the thre
classes of men. It is a parable. Three men hav
each acquired a large sum of money, and the
are not quite comfortable in their conscience a
to the way in which they got it. St. Ignatiu
simply says that their motive was not pure lov
of God, seeming to imply that the external ac
was not in itself wrong; it is not restitution c
which he is thinking, but of more perfect service
There is room for investigation; are they prepare
to carry out an impartial investigation, and t
abide by the results? Will they surrender th
money if the more perfect service of God demand

surrender? Well, about one of the parties there
can be no doubt. He means to keep that money.
Of course *he would like* to feel easy in conscience
about the matter, but there is never any real
chance of his taking action. Of the second man
there is more hope. His conscience is really
pricked; he realises that all is not as well as it
might be with his soul, and wishes to put matters
right. So he reflects and deliberates, and deliberates and reflects; but there is just one flaw
in it all. He contemplates with pleasure the
coming state of affairs, when he will be at perfect
peace with God, freed from all this anxiety — and
the money with him still. Somehow or other
that is always a feature in the picture. On that
point his mind is not really open, and he is
not indifferent. St. Ignatius well sums up this
second type when he says of him that he wishes
God to come his way and not himself to go to
God. It imports us greatly to see whether we
be really free and open-minded, or whether we
suffer from presuppositions. The third man really
wishes to rid himself of all presuppositions and
disordered affections. He wishes to serve God
alone, and the service of God is alone to decide
whether he keeps the money or no. Indeed, in
all things he wishes to have no other desire than
the divine service. This is true freedom, and
the perfection to which we should endeavour to
attain. But St. Ignatius, in accordance with

that fundamental rule of his spirituality that th
enemy is not merely to be beaten but to b
smashed, goes further still, like a very 'Houn
of Heaven'. If we feel within ourselves th
makings of a struggle, some repugnance t
something that God might ask of us, a desir
not to let something go, we are to protest t
God that we are ready and willing to mak
the sacrifice, and offer ourselves for that pur
pose to Him, if only such be His most hol
will. St. Ignatius is speaking of actual poverty
but the principle should evidently be extended
when the annual retreat brings up the questio
of reform.

THE THREE KINDS OF HUMILITY. This i
even more markedly a classification, not howeve
directly of types of men, but of states of soul
'Humility' is scarcely the word we should expec
to find applied to them; but St. Ignatius wishe
to insist on a certain common element in al
three, which is best represented by that word
He looks at it in this way: To what extent is ;
man prepared to humble and demean himself i
the service of God? How far is he preparec
to go on enduring all that is hard to mind anc
body?

The first kind of humility is necessary fo
eternal salvation. Not for anything in the worlc
would the man seriously deliberate about com
mitting a mortal sin. We may be tempted tc

hurry away from this kind as having no meaning for us. Yet that would be a mistake. We must reflect awhile how much it means for us to die in God's grace, and how weak we are apart from that same grace; we must beware of presumption, and always look upon ourselves as still capable of mortal sin. We may also think a little upon the sins of the world; even to confine ourselves to the present, how many of those who eagerly search their paper for some new sensation bethink them what an appalling output of offence against God its columns daily represent!

The second kind of humility consists in the attainment of that indifference for which we more particularly strove in the first week. This indifference, as we saw, consists primarily in the suspending of our choice, so long as the relation to God's service of what is to be chosen is not clear. Riches, honour, long life and the rest are no longer the object of our desire — that is, of our deliberate and intellectual desire, as opposed to mere natural inclination — save in so far as they may become means to God's greater service. And venial sin is held in utter horror, so that to save one's life one would not commit it. To be firmly established in this second kind of humility is already great holiness; indeed, it is practically impossible without at least frequent excursions into the third. And at the best no one can hope to be entirely free from indeliberate venial sins except by a most rare privilege, possibly never granted except to Our Blessed Lady.

But the third kind of humility is the most perfect. It includes the two preceding, yet goes far beyond them. Provided that no less praise and glory will accrue to the Divine Majesty, it prefers to be poor with Christ than to be rich, to suffer contempt and insult with Him, to be thought stupid with Him, rather than to have any name for wisdom and prudence. It understands the plan of Christ's campaign against the Devil, the World and the Flesh, and embraces it without reserve. We have here the true philosophy of the life of Christ as our great Exemplar, and of the religious life as a following of Him. Let us insist once more that it is not what St. Paul would call the death of the old man or of the flesh which is its supreme end, but union with Christ. The crucifixion of self is merely the necessary means to perfect union here below, and it is that union alone which makes such crucifixion possible or gives it a meaning. Hence it is not all darkness and misery, but rather the only sure peace and joy, because there is no longer a deadly struggle proceding within us for the mastery, but we are wholly Christ's, and one consoling glance of His makes every burden seem light. There can no more be any serious question of deliberate sin or imperfection. If the mere desire for God's greater glory should be sufficient to make us fulfil every duty of our day exactly and zealously, how much more the desire for Christ's cross, which makes us positively welcome all that such religious observance may cost us! The readiness, or at least the desire, to jump quickly and willingly at what they do not like is the sign of those who truly understand. Thus the third degree of humility is like oil to the wheels of organized effort, for there can be no friction with those who are filled with its spirit; and it makes for the most tremendous efficiency all along the line, because efficiency needs before all things the sacrifice of self. No doubt religious may at times be sensitive by nature, or self-assertive, or ambitious in the bad sense, and so of other tendencies of character, which do not depend upon them; but it is the third degree of humility which will prevent such temperaments from interfering with their service of God.

RESOLUTIONS. And now, if we have really filled ourselves with the spirit of the third man, or set of men, and with the third kind of humility, then we are ready to make the right sort of resolution. The consideration of the three classes of men inculcates thoroughness. Is it really obvious to us what God wants, or is it clear that a little trouble would make it obvious, and are we too feeble, too cowardly, to give it freely

and fully? Do we stand shivering on the ban
when one bold plunge would end the matte
We are not going to turn our backs upon Go
why, then, do we not turn them upon His fo
instead of shuffling between the two, and attemp
ing a miserable compromise? We must not l
content with half-measures in our resolution; on
we realise what is wanted, we must give it a
and more than all. If there is a fault to l
remedied, we must utterly smash it; if we hav
set a virtue before ourselves, both our ingenui
and our will-power must combine with grace
devise a course of action that will absolute
secure it.

And so with the third degree of humilit
If we are athirst for hardships, for insults ar
mockery, in a word, for all that could possib
frighten us away from making and meaning ar
keeping the right resolution, what is there th
can possibly hinder our perfection and holines.
But we must guard against delusion. In an annu
retreat of this kind we must not offer God tl
third degree of humility in general, but in tl
precise form in which He desires it. The sacrifi
must be the sacrifice He asks for; otherwise
will be beside the mark, and we shall be wastin
time and energy. If we have taken reasonab
care so far, and on the whole have been willir
and generous in our treatment of divine grac
and have earnestly endeavoured not to waste th

light granted us, but to use it to the full and act upon it, then we may be reasonably sure that our true cross for the year to come lies in our resolution. This we now finally determine and offer to God; we take up this cross willingly, because it is the cross of Christ, and He will bear it with us and for us.

EIGHTH DAY.

THE RESURRECTION.

PATRON: The Blessed Trinity.

READING: I Cor. XV; Apoc. XX, 11—XXII, 5; Imitation III, 5, 34.

FIRST MEDITATION: The Cross (The Divine Purpose, Asceticism, *Maria desolata*).

SECOND MEDITATION: The Resurrection (The Sinner in the City, The Apparition).

CONSIDERATION: Obedience (The Vow, The Virtue, Motives).

THIRD MEDITATION: The Kingdom of God (Teaching, Government, Ministry).

CONCLUSION: The Love of God (God's Benefits; God's Presence, Power and Essence; The Prayer).

✠

CAELESTIS URBS JERUSALEM.

O Heavenly City Jerusalem,
Of peace a blessed sight,
Which, wrought of living stones, art borne
Aloft to starry height,
While thousand thousand Seraphim
Engird thee with their flight!

O happy wedlock thine! His praise
The Father made thy dower:
The Spouse his grace about thee shed,
Fair consort of His power;
Yoke-fellow unto Christ the Prince
Art thou, the Heaven's bright tower.

Flung wide to all, thy gates shine forth
With many a gem most rare,
For virtue still doth point the way,
That he may thither fare,
Whoso, bestirred by Jesus' love,
Shall pain or hatred bear.

Fashioned with wholesome chiselling
And many a pounding blow,
With mason's hammering made smooth —
Thy stones are proven so,
And each to each in pinnacle
Together fitted show.

Unto the Father, the Most High,
The glory that is meet,
And to the Father's only Son,
And the great Paraclete;
Be praise, be power, be majesty
The while the ages fleet.   Amen.

EIGHTH DAY, FIRST MEDITATION:
THE CROSS.

THE Holy Eucharist and the Sacred Heart have already been considered as separate subjects of meditation; we have arrested our consideration of the historical sequence of events in order to give them our undivided and undistracted attention. Once more, now that we are come to the world's supreme tragedy, it seems best to adopt the same plan, and to concentrate our mind upon all that the Cross is to mean, rather than occupy it upon the single incidents in succession. These latter will provide valuable food for thought afterwards, and indeed those will find plenty of profit who prefer to consider them now; still, in a retreat it seems best to go straight to the heart of things, and to abstract from the actual history. Enough that we picture to ourselves the actual scene as accurately as we can. We stand beneath the Cross, gazing long and intently at the Crucified, trying to drink in ever deeper the tremendous lessons which such a spectacle brings home to us. Our Blessed Lady is there also, she who is herself learning no light lesson, more than ever before, who at the same time is the most perfect example of so much that needs to be mastered.

THE DIVINE PURPOSE. We may repeat here a good deal that we considered in the medi-

tation upon the Incarnation, in the third meditation of the fourth day, on the second point:
how Almighty God might have forgiven man
freely and without condition, or not have forgiven him at all: how in actual fact He decreed
that an adequate reparation should be offered
by His only-begotten Son: how Christ is not
merely our atonement, but our model. Here,
as we see Him upon the Cross, we may reflect
a little further upon the meaning of all this.
The least act of Christ was sufficient to make
the adequate reparation of which we have spoken,
because His least act possessed the infinite dignity
of His sacred Person. If, then, He suffered so
cruel an agony in the garden, if He was reviled
and outraged, slapped and spit upon, if His
innocent Flesh was torn with scourges and a
crown of thorns set upon His Head — all this
was not to make sure that enough satisfaction
was offered to His Father, but to bring home
to us the enormity of our offences. He gathered
up, as it were, in His own Person, He, the great
vicarious Sinner, the foulness of man's sins, and
the chastisement which they deserve. 'Him that
knew no sin, for us He hath made sin' (II Cor.
V, 21). Man thinks so lightly of sin; it is a
mere fillip to his jaded mind when he hears of
some more appalling outrage than usual against
the Divine Majesty. We ourselves make light
of our sins. It is left to Christ to make a tra-

gedy of them. It is the creature that stands to lose by sin, and thinks nothing of it; it is God that cannot be touched by it, and yet so utterly abhors it. Which view of it, then, are we to accept: the view of the man in the comfortable armchair, or the view of the God upon an infamous gibbet?

And Christ is also our own model. Much belongs here that is to be found in the beautiful chapter of the Imitation of Christ on the royal road of the Cross. A sovereign or other great personage when making a visit to some centre of population expects to be received in state, to say a few set words or perform some function, or then to have a departure arranged with equal state; and those who have been visited are stirred to enthusiasm and gratitude at the whole gracious act. Christ's plan was different. He came to sweeten and ennoble our suffering, and to teach us its true value. Suffering there must be; but there are many ways of bearing it. It may prove a great blessing, but also a great curse. With Christ and for Christ we can bear it cheerfully and well, and even rejoice, like the apostles (Acts V, 41), if we be found worthy to suffer for the Name of Jesus. Nay, we may seek suffering of our own accord, like the great St. Paul, who deliberately bruised his body and brought it into bondage (I Cor. IX, 27). Here, in short, with our eyes upon the Crucified and

His upon us, we may also repeat and more full
understand much that we considered in the thir
meditation of the seventh day, touching th
third degree of humility. If we would unit
ourselves with Christ, it must be upon His Cross
We cannot have Christ without the Cross, no
is the Cross worth anything without Christ upon
it. If St. Paul cries out, "Tis no longer I tha
live, 'tis Christ liveth in me', it is just after h
has told us: 'I am crucified with Christ' (Gal
II, 19-20).

ASCETICISM. Having said so much, let us de
velop a little more systematically what has been
said in the preceding point, and in the medita
tion alluded to. We may try to understand stil
more clearly both the doctrine and the practic
of asceticism, and the sight before us in thi
meditation will help at once to enlighten and to
encourage us. Let us look at the matter firs
from the point of view of reason. It is, indeed
a question whether Catholic asceticism can be
made fully intelligible to mere unaided reason
— there are mysteries in conduct, no less than
in articles of belief — but at least it seems pos
sible that reason should see that our ideal, i
realised, contains nothing fundamentally objection
able. And we can bring up concrete example
from the lives even of modern saints of something
very near the full attainment of the ideal, and
so recent a story as that of Gemma Galgani.

In the first place, then, it must be evident
that unless a man be prepared for suffering and
sacrifice, he cannot fulfil as he should what he
knows to be his duty. This is true of any man
in the world; it is doubly true of religious, whose
plain duty includes much that is contrary to
flesh and blood. Do not let us pass over this
aspect of the matter lightly, for indeed it would
mean very great holiness not to be wanting
herein. To attend to our spiritual duties and
all our other work punctually, to bestow a reasonable care upon them, to bear patiently the
various trials that come our way unasked, to
be cheerful in charity and obedience — all these
things argue a very mortified soul, and yet there
is no voluntary seeking of pain or humiliation
about them. It would be a great mistake, therefore, to set great store only upon those morti-
fications which are due to our own initiative;
plenty will come unasked, and we should be
perfect indeed if we bore them all as we should.
Only it may well be questioned whether this be
even remotely probable without some voluntary
mortification on our part. And so we come to
the second consideration, that the self-schooled
man is better able both to endure what may
befall him and to undertake what is difficult.
He is already in training for the task that will
demand constant self-denial, perhaps heroic patience or heroic effort. Clearly, the more that

we are capable of in this respect, the more we
may hope to do for God; that is a truth to
the application of which there is practically
no limit. What seems hard, or too hard, is
largely a relative term; it depends, so to speak,
upon our degree of training. And again, a severer training of self in this respect, as has already been implied, means an easier resistance
to sin all along the line, but especially in the
matter of the sixth commandment; that is a principle upon which St. Paul himself acted (I Cor.
IX, 27). Where, then, are we to set the limit
to this 'chastising of the body'? Where indeed,
save in our own power of endurance? But this
latter must be taken in a wide sense, not only
as comprising the avoidance of anything like
serious injury to the body, but also the mainten-
ance of a proper disposition of mind. Any practice of penance is mistaken which tends to prey
seriously and constantly upon the soul, to rob
it of peace and joy and love. But if these can
be shown to remain, even the man of the world
will hardly blame or despise such a cheerful
bearing of the Cross.

Such motives, then, are in a manner philosophical, and as here explained at least carry
great weight with mere human reason, however much the religious life as a whole may
be a puzzle to it, if unaided by faith, or even
darkened by agnosticism. Yet faith adds two

further considerations of its own, without weakening those set forth above. It bids us do penance for our sins, and even, after the example of Christ Himself, for others also. We find this a constant practice in the Old Testament, where, we may remark, voluntary penance was especially common in the form of fasting; and it really finds some foundation in the instincts of nature. And there is the example of Christ Our Lord. He has set the example, He has mapped out the campaign; it would be enough for us merely to know that, for He is Infinite Wisdom and Infinite Love. And so the saints have understood Him; in loving Him they have also loved the Cross, or rather, and here we come back more directly to the picture before us, it is upon the Cross that He Himself has most won their love. 'And I, if I be lifted up from the earth, will draw all things to myself' (John XII, 32).

Maria desolata. It is a pious practice in the Church to pass from the more direct contemplation of the suffering of Christ to the spectacle of His Mother, silently sorrowing beneath the Cross. Much that we have learnt from the sight of the Son is reinforced, and the sight of the Mother also brings some new thoughts. We naturally dwell first upon what strikes us at once most forcibly. Mary is beholding the suffering of her Son. She is taking it all in, drinking it in, we might say; and by that very fact she is

become the Queen of Martyrs. For it is no
idle regret or hysterical excitement that fills he
soul. 'Behold the handmaid of the Lord!' Said
once at Nazareth, it has never been revoked
Mary was ready for all that might be included
in that supreme act of submission to the Divine
Will. And indeed, this is the culmination of a
past already long. We have seen something of
her sorrows. Even before the birth of her Di
vine Son, she must have understood the tor
turing perplexity in which her state placed St. Jo
seph, a perplexity of which she could only leave
God Himself to explain the sublime cause. And
Simeon had prophesied that a sword should
pierce her heart. We may think of her other
troubles, or else come at once to the realisation
of that prophecy. We may say that the lance
that pierced the Saviour's side was the sword
that transfixed His Mother's heart. No mother
could feel the love and veneration for her son
that Mary felt for Jesus, and it is through these
most holy feelings that the pain comes to her
And she welcomes it as a part of the great di
vine scheme, even as she would not have her
Son elsewhere than on the Cross.

As she is minded touching the present and
the past, so she is also minded with regard to
the future. She knows for whom her Son is
suffering; she has taken in all that the Cross
means, and made it her own: Christ had said

much on the point to His disciples, and we can but suppose that she had turned over these things, too, in her mind. If her Son is dying for sinners, she unites herself with Him in that offering of Himself, and her own sufferings are for sinners also. And we may believe that as after the Annunciation she came to realise more and more fully the significance of the Divine Motherhood, so here she was enlightened as to the meaning of the new maternity which Christ bestowed upon her from the Cross. Beneath the Cross she is enduring the pangs of this second motherhood, and those very pangs are the pledge of her love for those who have cost her so much, and whom she recognises are her children from the Lord. As they are to be one with Christ, it follows that it is part of the divine scheme that they are to be children of hers. With thoughts such as these in our mind, we may ponder over the *Stabat Mater* and recite it slowly, steeping ourselves in sympathy with Mary in her desolation.

EIGHTH DAY, SECOND MEDITATION:

THE RESURRECTION.

When we are meditating upon the end for which we were created, and upon our plain duty in life, or later upon our sins and the punishment they deserve, or later still upon the life

17 *

of Christ and all that it should mean for us,
we see more and more clearly what there is to
amend in our lives, but the thought must inevitably come to us, that to carry out this re-
formation will cost us something. And so it must;
for a resolution that demands no efforts and no
self-sacrifice is not worth having. But for that
effort and that self-sacrifice we are to find our
hope and strength in the Passion of Christ, which
is next propounded to us. Christ has won us
the grace, has shown us the way, has sweetened
our cross; and we are asked to do far less for
Him than He has done for us. The Passion is
the first answer to that presentiment, that it will
be hard; the Resurrection is the second, of a
supplementary character. The thought of what
Christ has suffered is to make us ready, and
even eager, to suffer for Him and with Him;
the thought of His triumph is to remind us that
if we suffer with Him, we shall also be glorified
with Him (Rom. VIII, 17), that it is His triumph
which awaits us, or rather is already working in
us, for 'in all these things we overcome because
of Him that hath loved us' (Rom. VIII, 37). Christ
was delivered up for our sins, as the Apostle
says, and rose again for our justification (Rom.
IV, 25). True, it was His death that atoned once
for all for our sins, and brought us justification,
and therefore our redemption comes from Calvary; but it is in and with the risen Christ that

the justified rise from their sins in the inchoate glory of a new life, they are His glorious members, and He communicates to them abundantly His own divine life (Rom. VI, 1—11, etc.). It is the risen Christ, in short, that is our supernatural life, and in this sense our abiding justification; it is no longer we who live, but the risen Lord that liveth in us (Gal. II, 20). In winning glory for Himself, He has also won it for us.

All these thoughts are suitable now, but to give them body and force it appears best to take one especial apparition, and reflect upon that. It is natural to take the first recorded, at all events in St. John's gospel, that to the Magdalen. St. Ignatius in his Spiritual Exercises takes it for granted that Our Blessed Lord appeared first to His own beloved Mother. She alone, we may well suppose, awaited with unshaken faith His resurrection, and, if we please, we may dwell upon that first meeting. And yet, how difficult to imagine it! For ourselves, seeing there is but one apparition to be considered, we may essay the humbler task of pondering over details already supplied by the gospel text. Even this latter course, however, is not without a certain difficulty, and we must make two presuppositions. Firstly, that, to put it in that way, there is only one Magdalen; there are three characters in the gospel that cannot be identified with absolute certainty, namely, Mary the sister of Lazarus

and Martha, Mary Magdalen, and the 'sinner in
the city' of Luke VII, 37, but it seems most prob
able that they are all one and the same. The
present writer has given his reasons for think
ing so in an article entitled 'The Sinner in the
City', which appeared in the *Expositor* for July
1909; this is no place to discuss the question
at length, but it is right to mention that the
identification is here assumed, although not beyond all question. Secondly, it must even more
evidently be assumed that the gospel accounts
of Easter morning can be reconciled one with
another. It may be worth while to remind ourselves that the proof of the resurrection cannot
in strictness be said to depend upon this being
done. Had we an enquirer who was prepared
to admit miracles upon reasonable evidence, we
might point out to him the convergent testimony
of the gospels, and indeed of the New Testament generally, upon the central facts, and we
might reasonably demand that, even if he per-
sisted in believing that there are inconsistencies
of detail, he should still look upon such inconsistencies as no more than natural, considering
the confusion and intense excitement that prevailed upon that first Easter morning. But we,
who in the light of the Church's teaching believe
that there are no real contradictions in Holy
Writ, naturally attempt to weave a consistent
narrative out of all the materials with which the

gospels supply us. The attempt may be made
in various ways, but does not concern us here.
Practically it will be enough, in following St. John's
narrative, to abstract from that of the other
evangelists. On the other hand, if we are to
attempt to fathom the true significance of the
apparition to the Magdalen, we must take account of her previous history, and of all that
Christ had meant to her before. We must understand how much seemed lost, before we can in
any way grasp the joy that took possession
of her.

THE SINNER IN THE CITY (Luke VII, 36—50).
As has already been said, we assume that the
woman who appears in this episode is the Magdalen. She was at this time a public sinner, her
infamy was notorious. None, indeed, had better
cause to know it than Simon the Pharisee, if, as
we may suppose, he is to be identified with
Simon the leper (Matt. XXVI, 6); in that case it
seems likely from John XII, 1—8, that he was
a relation of the Magdalen, possibly her father,
and doubtless regarded her as a disgrace to the
family. So, indeed, she then was; but he himself was at fault too, for, like the rest of his
kind, he had forgotten mercy (Matt. XXIII, 23),
and probably had made little effort to save the
lost sheep. It was not the Pharisees' way to attempt to convert sinners. But women of that
kind are sometimes keenly alive to the ignominy

of their position, and also show themselves capable at times of generous impulses; so that they still stand a better chance than many a Pharisee (Matt. XXI, 31). And the Magdalen had doubtless been deeply moved, perhaps at first by the Baptist, but at all events when she had read in the eyes of Christ all the love and compassion with which He was awaiting her. Perhaps it was curiosity that had first drawn her to listen, perhaps a flippant sneer was on her lips; perhaps, again, she was there when Christ expounded the parable of the Prodigal Son, meaning to speak to her own heart above all. She understood; and overwhelming shame and repentance battled with the ardent desire to cast herself entirely upon Him who alone could save her.

Simon had apparently been cured of leprosy. It was a little thing, compared to what Christ had done for the Magdalen; and so he 'loved little' (Luke VII, 47). Perhaps he felt obliged to invite Our Lord to his house; but he was still a Pharisee at heart, and it was no very kind welcome that he gave Him. He may have thought that Our Lord would not notice his omission of the usual offices of hospitality or friendship, or noticing them, would be only too glad to avail Himself of such an honourable invitation even at that price. He must have been not a little disconcerted when Our Lord brought

up his discourteous treatment, point by point,
to contrast him with the Magdalen, in application of His parable. For indeed he had never
reckoned that his disreputable relative would
make his invitation the occasion of coming back
to her family, and when Our Lord made no protest against the scene she was making, Simon in
amazed indignation made up his mind that this
decided the matter; none of these gutter-prophets
for him! 'If he knew!' Christ did know; and He
who justified the publican rather than that other
Pharisee, had found one who was to love him,
it may be, more than all other women, excepting
only His Blessed Mother. And what did He think
of Simon? His vigorous defence of the Magdalen
was also a mercy to him who had judged her
so unjustly, a mercy that we may suppose from
later events accepted. Simon, too, forgave the
Magdalen; if ever he came to think that he needed forgiveness from her, it was not, we may
be sure, because she herself ever pressed such
a consideration upon him. Her only wish was
to be at Jesus' feet, her only thought for what
was indeed 'the best portion' (Luke X, 42), her
love calmer now, yet ever deepening. Thus she
would sit and listen to His words — or was it
not enough sometimes, and more than enough,
to be there in silence? She had found indeed
one whom her soul could love, and would not
let him go (Canticle of Canticles III, 4).

THE APPARITION. Such a beginning we should pass before our mind, if we would understand in any faint degree the Magdalen's feelings upon this Easter morning. What a passion of woe had been hers, and still was upon her! With what a crash all her hopes had come to the ground! Vague those hopes had been, no doubt, yet one feature was always there: the Master, calm and yet earnest, affectionate and yet so full of heavenly dignity: and at His feet — herself. And yet, she could not think it had been fraud or delusion, every fibre of her being protested against such an idea. And on the other hand, she had not understood — had not understood so much that Christ had said or done for her, had not understood that she herself had already forestalled His death (Matt. XXVI, 12, etc.), in part fulfilling an office that would only be imperfectly executed for lack of time, when that death came — she had not sufficiently understood even the raising of Lazarus, in spite of all that Christ had said upon that occasion to stir up faith. Like the disciples journeying to Emmaus, she had had her *sperabamus* (Luke XXIV, 21), glorious hopes that now seemed so vain, hopes that here was the true Saviour of Israel. And now what could she think? Nevertheless, once more like those disciples who could not help bursting forth into praise of Crist, at a time when it was scarcely safe to do so, she also retained her love, indeed it seems only to have burnt the more fiercely by reason of her grief and disappointment. First she runs to tell Peter and John that Christ's Body had been removed; they do not believe her, until they have run to the tomb and looked for themselves. Then, if we may modernise the incident a little, like practical men they go home and have their breakfast. Why not, indeed? It seemed the only thing to do. And yet it is not common sense that Our Lord is in search of, or even a sense of humour, valuable as these things are in their measure. It was the unreasoning love of the Magdalen that won His first favour — always excepting, as has been said, His Blessed Mother — and we may surely see a delicate reproof in His sending through her His first message to His apostles. And thus it has been through the history of His Church; to take what is in a manner a crowning example, there were many learned theologians who might have been inspired to found the devotion to the Sacred Heart, yet it was the ardent but unsophisticated love of St. Margaret Mary in which He placed His good pleasure, and His message came through her. Human wisdom, after all, is but folly before God; it was love that brought Christ upon earth, and it is love that He seeks in return.

And Christ shows His love to the Magdalen with a playful delicacy. Angels she saw, and took no thought for them, nor indeed of the Lord of angels, possibly because He disguised His voice, even as He disguised His appearance to the disciples going to Emmaus; but the Magdalen's preoccupation, far as she was from expecting anything of the sort, may be enough to account for her not recognising Him. Others, again, suppose that she was beside herself in suggesting that she could carry Christ's Body alone; but then she may have relied on getting help. Be that as it may, no further mistake was possible when she heard her own name spoken, and spoken as Christ alone could speak it, in a tone rich with God's love for His own chosen soul. How she started! With a sudden gasp she turned, and there was Christ, quietly smiling at her as before, almost as if nothing had happened. And yet there was a difference; He was marked with the five wounds, and something perhaps of the glory now proper to His Body may have shown through. In a measure we may apply to Him what St. Paul says of the glorified body of the just in general, such as it is to be: 'What is sown in corruption doth rise in incorruption; what is sown in dishonour doth rise in glory; what is sown in weakness doth rise in power; what is sown a natural body doth rise a spiritual body' (I Cor. XV, 42—44). But the Magdalen has no eye for these things; she is already at His feet. 'Touch me not!' She needs a gentle reminder. The old life is after all to be no more; she is filled with His divine consolations, but their old intimacy is only to be taken up in heaven, when He has ascended, when she too has left this world. It is not His purpose to begin anew His former life, but only to fulfil a definite work before ascending — to comfort and instruct His own, and to prepare the way for His Church.

EIGHTH DAY, CONSIDERATION:

OBEDIENCE.

Obedience is the virtue of the soldier. We kindle with enthusiasm as we read of its supreme practice:

> Theirs not to make reply,
> Theirs not to reason why,
> Theirs but to do, and die!

The more religious obedience is examined, the more it will be found in accord with resolves such as these, which arouse general admiration. Yet men shrink from the cold-blooded analysis even of their noblest ideals, and when the same thing is presented to them, no longer in stirring reality, but in the abstract, and in language perhaps a little technical, they may pass from warm applause to silence and distrust. Such an analysis, however, there must be, if in our quest after perfection we are to choose with care and deliberation what is best. Only, there is no need to part from the popular ideal and all that it implies, strong habits of discipline, a regard not only for the spirit but also for the letter of the law, the strenuous and unquestioning execution of orders, unswerving loyalty to all those in authority and to the service in general. We have here, not only efficient accomplishment, but a readiness, almost an eagerness, to believe alike in commander and command. And it is significant that our people love to think of this ideal as being realised in those branches of the public service which not only have to face most difficulty and danger in their behalf, but on whose efficiency everything depends. The greater the obstacles and perils, the more important the work to be done, so much the greater need there is, not only of capable leaders, but of implicit obedience being paid to them. And if it be true that a capable leader may so manage matters as to prevent mistakes or insubordination on the part of those under him from having serious consequences, it is still truer that a prompt and faithful obedience will again and again have a successful issue where the measures were really less wise in themselves. For the present to keep this model before our eyes will help us to clear and practical ideas; though our ultimate model can only be Christ Our Lord.

THE VOW. Obedience may be defined as the virtue which moves the subject to accomplish

he known will of his superior. The superior's
ight to obedience is based in the first place,
f he be a priest, on ecclesiastical jurisdiction in
he strict sense, and in any case he has the right
which is founded on the vow of obedience. That
free offering which the religious made of himself, gave lawful superiors the right to command
him. It was founded upon a deliberate conviction
that God had called him to the religious state,
a conviction shared by those who were best
qualified to judge, and who knew the responsibility they were taking upon themselves, both
towards God, the order and the individual. And
that offering was recognised by all as irrevocable
on the part of the religious. His obedience,
therefore, is no longer founded directly upon
the sense of a divine call. Doubtless that sense
will remain and grow stronger; but it should be
remembered that, even if it disappear, the duty
of obedience remains, and a dispensation is necessary to remove it. Where the interest of the
individual demands this, the interest of the order
will also lie that way; but the possibility of
such a dispensation does not prevent the tie
from being in a true sense absolute, irrevocable,
founded only indirectly upon the God-given call,
directly upon the solemn promise which, as has
been set forth in the third meditation of the
second day, goes to make of religion a permanent and stable state.

In orders such as that of the Friars Preachers and of the Society of Jesus, where the rule does not of itself bind under sin, it is clear that an offence against the rule can only become sinful by reason of some ulterior obligation, such as the commandments of God or the Church, or the vows. Where the rule binds under sin, a good deal depends how this is understood. The living superior, in the next place, may or may not wish to impose an obligation under sin. As far as he is concerned, a mortal sin against the vow of obedience can only be committed in two ways, by the rejection either of the command, or of the whole principle of authority. In the rejection of the command it is committed when some adequate authority, such as the local superior, clearly manifests the intention to induce an obligation of this kind, commanding in such terms as according to the constitutions and customs of the order put the matter beyond doubt. It is also essential that what is commanded be no trifle, but something of serious import, for otherwise there can be no serious obligation in respect of it. A mortal sin is also committed when the principle of obedience is itself rejected, by a formal contempt of the superior's authority as such. This is not a very likely case, but it should be noticed that an answer, 'I won't', or the like phrase, will usually be of the nature of a serious contempt, and constitutes a grave injury to the superior in his official capacity.

When venial sin is committed depends upon the obligation intended by the rule, if this bind under sin at all, or by the superior. The latter may or may not wish to impose an obligation under sin, as the case may be; but if he do impose this obligation, there is always the further sin against the vow. At all events the great mass of authors, both ancient and modern, hold that every sin of disobedience, whether to rule or superior, is also a sin against the vow. The only difficulty in the matter comes from the 'norms' or fundamental rules issued by the Sacred Congregation of Bishops and Regulars in 1901, where it is laid down that 'a sister is only bound to obey in virtue of her vow when her lawful superior expressly orders her in virtue of holy obedience, or under formal precept, or in words equivalent, according to the constitutions. It is further advisable that the formal command be imposed in writing, or at least before two witnesses.' This in any case would only have direct reference to future institutes of simple vows; but even in their regard it seems unlikely that the Sacred Congregation meant to throw overboard the common consent of the standard authorities, and its decree is doubtless to be understood to refer to the obligation to obey under mortal sin, this being by far the more important issue.

There remains the case in which it is plain
that the superior would like something to be
done, although he has not given any command
on the point. Evidently in this case there can
be no question of sin, nor of the vow, nor of
any strict obligation, but only of the more perfect
practice of the virtue, which will generally lie in
the execution of such wishes. This case, however,
must not be confused with that of compliance
with the rules. Even when these latter do not
bind under sin, they induce a true obligation,
being true laws, and the superior may bind the
subject in conscience to submit to a penance for
a breach of them, which, however, he is certainly
not understood to wish to do in the case of
slighter penances. Further, as has been pointed
out, what appears to be a mere breakage of rule
may easily bring some slight sin along with it,
by reason of some fault in the motive; but in
that case the vow will not add to the guilt. If
the vow be solemn, the sin will doubtless be
somewhat more serious, because, as has been
said above, the bond which the religious would
weaken or snap is closer; but an otherwise venial
sin can never become mortal on this account,
nor does law or custom attach any special dis-
abilities to the solemn vow.

If an objection to what we are ordered should,
after prayer on the subject, appear to us worthy of
mention, it is our duty to make a representation

on the subject, but we should be prepared, so
far as is reasonably possible, to give the superior's
ruling our fullest adhesion. For fear of giving
a handle to the ill-disposed, or to those who know
nothing of the Church or of religious life, it may
be well to add another proviso, though it will
not be needed by others, namely, that there can
never be any obligation to sin. If the subject
is reasonably certain that a command contains
sin, he must not obey it; if there be real doubt,
the superior should have the benefit of it, though
a representation may be made and, under normal
circumstances, advice sought from one's confessor
or others. Indeed, it would be well to do this
in any case.

THE VIRTUE. Having thus spoken at some
length about the vow, there is less need to dilate
upon the subject of the virtue, especially as the
introductory remarks are largely concerned with
it, and indeed the last point in this consideration
also. And then, the well-known letter of St. Ignatius has become the classic treatment of the
subject, and those who would go deeper into
the subject cannot do better than study it carefully. Here it will be enough to touch upon a
certain number of points which appear to illustrate
well the general spirit in which obedience should
be rendered. Above all things, it is necessary
to see God in our superiors, 'not looking to the
things that are seen, but to the things that are not

18 *

seen' (II Cor. IV, 18). On this subject something
was said in the first meditation of the second day.
To see God in the superior in this way means
that we shall be ready to do anything that we
know he seriously wishes as superior to have
done, whether that knowledge come to us by
way of an order or no; indeed, it may be said
in general that they are most obedient who need
fewest orders. And again, they also who need
least in the way of explanations and information.
Superiors may be too reticent, just as they may
be too communicative, but it is never good to
set to work to 'pump' them, and least of all
where there is question of an act of obedience.
There may be something that we feel we need
to have explained to us, and we may represent
the fact, but ultimately it is for the superior to
judge how much we are to be told, and we
should acquiesce in his judgment. It is a blessed
thing to be able to work well in harness, and
under such restrictions as obedience may impose,
without making preliminary conditions as to the
amount of freedom in our work we are to enjoy,
the degree of confidence to be shown us, and
so forth. Even if all these things be not as we
should wish, our obedience should in no way
depend upon them, and we should take the
greatest care not to put ourselves, as it were,
into opposition, especially when older. On the
contrary, we should have every consideration for

superiors, not merely being loyal but even kind
to them so far as we can, avoiding, too, anything
like victimising them. We should study their
convenience, remembering that subjects are many
while superiors are one, and reckoning with the
possibility, or probability, that others may make
the same demands upon superiors' time and trouble
as ourselves. Sometimes what wears them out
are the things 'that won't give any trouble'.

None can fail to recognise that obedience is due
to those who are commonly called 'superiors'
simply, such as the superior of the house, and
perhaps one or two of the chief officials; but it
may be more difficult to give a proper obedience
to those in subordinate offices, who only have
a very limited sphere of action entrusted to them.
Yet, as far as it actually is entrusted to them, they
have authority to carry out what is reasonably
necessary, and, it may be, to make certain demands
upon others, with which true obedience demands
compliance. It may be worth while, however,
for all such to reflect that it is their business
to get the work done as efficiently and smoothly
as possible, without taking occasion to form a
court or endeavouring to make their own little
corner the hub of the universe. It is possible
to magnify one's office in a wrong way; the best
worker, like the best servant, is often he who
attracts least attention. Again, the same spirit of
faith that is zealous in obedience to minor officials

will also find the voice of God in the ringing of
the bell, and other such signals; punctuality is
a very practical form of the virtue.

So much depends upon cultivating the right
frame of mind, that acquiescence in all direction
that comes from God which we call blind obedience.
It is a release from many troubles, and a sure
way to peace and joy. Let us thank God that
it is not our duty to thrash out the *pro's* and
con's of all things, and let us credit those whose
duty it is with being at least as capable as
ourselves, and having the help of God besides.
Let us dread playing the part of the superior
person, the habit of scorn and criticism. Rather
in this perhaps we may hope to improve upon
the military ideal, that while the soldier is quick
to obey the word of command when it comes,
the religious, quick and ready in all things to
discern the will of God, makes the word of
command unnecessary, forestalling, with alert yet
prudent instinct, all that might be asked of him.

MOTIVES. Even at the expense of leaving some
part of the subject untouched, such as the checks
imposed by obedience in the way of leaves and
the correction of faults, we must hurry on to
a brief consideration of some of the motives upon
which the practice of it rests. We may mention
four. In the first place, there is the practical
motive. This has been sufficiently illustrated in
the introduction to the meditation. Or instead of

looking to the soldier and sailor, we might look to any great business organization, and remind ourselves that every such institution must have its acting manager, that the hands are there to work, and not to indulge in long and careful deliberations best left to the few and the wise, that efficiency depends largely on loyal co-operation, and so forth. Then, there is the motive of necessity. Perhaps obedience is the only virtue which is almost bound to become more difficult as we grow older. The novice easily takes things on faith, but as he is moved into positions of responsibility and feels surer of his ground, he more easily developes views of his own. Again, obedience brings all other virtues along with it, and entire submission to the rule and to superiors is thus the short cut to perfection. Finally, there is the example of Christ, who became obedient unto death, even unto death upon a cross.

EIGHTH DAY, THIRD MEDITATION:

THE KINGDOM OF GOD.

In the Acts of the Apostles we are told that after His resurrection Our Lord for forty days kept appearing to His apostles and used to speak to them of what concerned the Kingdom of God. It will not be amiss, therefore, that at this stage of our retreat we too should reflect upon God's kingdom on earth, which is the Church, that we

should make of our Easter joy a Pentecostal joy
also. It is evident that a religious must not
conclude a retreat without reflecting seriously
upon his attitude towards the Church, to ask
himself whether he venerates her sufficiently as
the source of Divine truth, whether he accepts
her teaching and her government loyally, whether
he appreciates the unspeakable dignity of the
sacred priesthood and of the mysteries of God.
The high value which he sets upon the call to
the religious life must not lessen, but rather
increase, his esteem of the common heritage, the
rock upon which religious life is built.

The Church may be said to have been in-
stituted by degrees. Under the Old Covenant
the prophets did not receive their mission from
the official hierarchy, but directly from God.
The Baptist was the last and greatest of the
prophets; he closed the old dispensation and
prepared the way for the new, but did not himself
belong to this latter. 'The least in the Kingdom
of Heaven is greater than he' (Matt. XI, 11). But
as soon as Christ, in the fulness of His power,
began to make disciples, and much more when
He sent them out to preach, He was commencing
the formation of a new religious society, the
sufficient authority for whose existence was to be
found in Himself. It was the legitimate development of the previous, the Old Testament society,
but not in any ordinary sense identically one

with it. We can trace various stages in the evolution of the new organisation, such as the raising of the apostles to the priesthood at the Last Supper, and the commission to preach to the whole world given after the resurrection; but we had best picture now to ourselves the completion of the process, the descent of the Holy Ghost upon the apostles in the form of fiery tongues. After that the Church was in a manner equipped even more fully than at present; for the apostles possessed individually the gift of infallibility in their public teaching and, not to speak of other peculiar privileges, were capable of receiving fresh revelations so long as they lived, whereas at the death of the last apostle the deposit of faith was closed, and now there is but one who possesses the gift of individual infallibility, the Vicar of Christ.

TEACHING. The truth of the Church's teaching is guaranteed both by the infallibility of the Church herself, and by the infallibility of her visible Head upon earth. When the *Ecclesia docens* as a whole is regularly and normally teaching a doctrine as part of the deposit of faith, and therefore binding upon the faithful, that doctrine is infallibly true. By the *Ecclesia docens* we here understand the Catholic episcopate taken collectively, with the Holy Father in his proper place at their head — not necessarily all the bishops without exception, but a sufficient number to make a moral whole. And the Holy Father

himself, when as supreme ruler of the Church
upon earth he defines a doctrine to be held by
all as an article of faith, is also an infallible
exponent of the content of Revelation, not by
reason of the acceptance of the definition by the
Church, but in virtue of the prerogative attached
by Christ to his own office. Again, this infallibility of Church and Pope has existed down
from the time of Christ, so that wherever it has
clearly expressed itself, there also Catholics find
matter for an irrevocable intellectual assent.

Holy Writ, too, is of course infallible; but it
should be remembered that the Church had existed
complete in itself for several years before even
a word of the New Testament had been written,
that it is the Church alone that can teach us
what works actually constitute the Sacred Scrip-
tures, and that there is no doctrine more un-
scriptural than the doctrine which teaches that
'Holy Scripture containeth all things necessary to
salvation' (art. 6 of the Anglican articles), if this
be understood to mean either that there is no
need of a living teacher, or that the living teacher
is only to be heard so far as he can prove from
the Bible what he asserts. As a matter of fact,
Scripture, no less than Tradition, bids us turn
for actual guidance, not to the written word, but
to the living teacher.

Far be it from us to be of the number of
those, if such there be, who make no account

of the teaching of Pope or Church except where they are infallible; it is evident that such an attitude is not loyal, that we must always do our best to obey and to accept all that comes to us from such a source. Still, in a short presentation of the subject such as this we may be content to confine our attention more or less to the actual deposit of faith. Nothing is more worth knowing or more worth teaching than that; it is the supreme truth and the supreme guide of life, and experience only shows how wide a gap and how unfathomable a craving is in the soul that is without it. It is a source of a peace and repose beyond compare, because it brings with it the secure possession of what millions are tormenting themselves to find. It is also a source of unparalleled strength and energy; because all the so called miracles of science, or in general of organisation, accomplish nothing compared to the steady and often heroic output of the true faith. We see it in the lives of priest and people, in the magnificent sacrifices made by the laity for their religion, in the devotion with which multitudes of men and women consecrate their whole lives to the more perfect and immediate service of God. But this is a theme to which we can here do no justice.

GOVERNMENT. It is not the Church's function merely to proclaim divine truth, like the prophets of old, without any further commission; she enjoys, not only the power to teach, but the power to govern. She possesses an external organisation, wherein some are rulers, and some are ruled, making up together a complete hierarchy. She is an independent society held together by an authority subject to none upon earth, which comprises within itself the right of legislation, judicature and executive — of making laws, of judging offences against them, of administrative action. It is the one characteristic common to all the bodies that have fallen away from her, that they have not been able to produce any satisfactory doctrine of authority; with them the so-called Church has very often become a mere department of the State. And so the need and principle of authority has long been a fruitful source of conversions to the Catholic Church; what is laid down so clearly in the New Testament, what our very common sense and the experience of history teaches to be so necessary, they have found in the Church, and they have marvelled at the vast multitude who in every nation obey their pastors, and above all their supreme pastor, and derive from their humble submission to teaching and government incredible consolation and zealous enthusiasm. The Church, indeed, is not for the Pope, but the Pope for the Church; even in the natural order man would have need of an external religious system — he must worship in body no less than in spirit, and as a member of society no less than as an individual — but all this requires a strong central authority, and as a matter of fact Christ has endowed that authority with ample powers. The faithful, then, march shoulder to shoulder in glorious array, but their loyalty to their great cause and to each other springs from their loyalty to their Divine Commander, Christ, which also of necessity brings with it loyalty to His Vicar upon earth, and to all who hold jurisdiction in the Church. Thus the Church is an organic body, the Mystical Body of Christ, one with Him, because she is permeated with His divine life; she is the vine, the kingdom of God, the new Jerusalem.

We cannot esteem too highly our place in this Body of Christ; but our esteem must take on a practical shape. We may note that when the Apostle propounds the doctrine of the Mystical Body, he usually does it with a view to inculcating proper subordination, contentment with one's own appointed place in the grand organism. Superiors, bishops, the pope, are all to receive the honour and obedience due to them. The Holy Father is, indeed, the ultimate superior of all religious, and of course has a far greater right than any other to all that is due from subject to superior. We may leave it to an ill-informed and prejudiced press to make the brilliant discovery at frequent intervals that Rome has finally betrayed and exposed herself; we shall remain

loyal, and try according to our measure to know
what to say, and decline to swell the hapless
ranks of the disgruntled.

MINISTRY. Besides the power to teach and
govern, Our Lord committed to His Church the
sacred ministry, the power of sacrament and
sacrifice, the most sacred power of all, for which
to a large extent the other two may be said to
exist. Baptism any one may validly administer,
and it is the faithful themselves, the parties being
married, that, strictly speaking, are the ministers
of the sacrament of Matrimony. Any one, too,
may validly administer the sacrament of the Holy
Eucharist, but the power to consecrate, the power
to offer the sacrifice, belongs to priests alone,
to whom also appertains the administration of
Penance and Extreme Unction. Mere priests may
receive power to confirm, and to confer minor
orders, and even the subdiaconate, but the power
to confer the diaconate and priesthood is absolutely confined to bishops. The Holy Father, it
may be noticed, from the point of view of ministerial power as such is a bishop and no more;
there is no special sacrament which he alone can
administer.

The whole life of our soul depends upon this
ministerial power. It was Baptism that first produced sanctifying grace, the Christ-life of the
soul, within us. For those, too, who have been
raised to the singular dignity of the priesthood,

the reception of that sacrament must appear as admission to a new and far higher life; and the other sacraments have their special function and their special beauty. But in the ordinary course of our lives it is the Holy Eucharist and the sacrament of Penance that support us and most claim our attention. The latter helps us to correct our faults and sins, after a proper scrutiny of our lives; its chief function is to remove all that is evil or imperfect. The Holy Eucharist, as a sacrament, is Christ Himself, come to us to be unspeakably united to us, to take entire possession of our whole self. And we should make it the whole endeavour of our lives, to keep nothing back from Him, to abandon ourselves utterly to Him, when He comes to us. And when He comes to us, He comes to us through the ministry of the priests of the Church, a ministry which we can never sufficiently esteem, and for which we can never be sufficiently grateful to her Divine Founder.

CONCLUSION:

THE LOVE OF GOD.

We have now come to the grand finale of the retreat, the direct attempt to attain to what is most perfect and most sublime. There can be no limit to our attempt, we can never have too much of the love of God, and it can never be too pure and disinterested. Yet this does not mean that we can afford henceforth to occupy ourselves with nothing else; the strength of our love of God depends to a large extent upon our hold on all that leads up to that love. At the present time, for instance, we have thought well about the last things, we have contemplated Our Lord's life and death and resurrection in all the significance that it bears for us, its lesson of love in suffering and of triumph through the Cross; by every means in our power we have purified our hearts and attached them to Christ — all this we need to do and, little by little, far more, and we need to do it constantly, if our love of God is to thrive.

At the outset of the contemplation, St. Ignatius bids us notice two things. In the first place, love consists rather in deeds than in words. In the second place, it expresses itself in the communication by the lover to the one beloved of what he has, or of what he can give in other ways. St. Ignatius instances the communication of knowledge or honours or wealth. These two remarks are meant to guide us in our subsequent reflections. Wishing as we do to obtain a full and calm conviction that God loves us, we must examine what He has done for us, and how He communicates Himself to us; and we in our turn must not delude ourselves with the mechanical use of expressions of ardent devotion, but must ask ourselves what we are really doing or mean to do, and must abandon ourselves utterly to Him who is Love itself. Words and deeds should go together.

St. Ignatius would have us picture ourselves standing before God and His angels and saints, who are praying for us. This is a peculiarly solemn *mise-en-scène* for the meditation; it is only used once previously in the Exercises, namely, in the meditation on the three classes of men, which in this retreat is included in the third meditation of the seventh day. It may be said to reappear in the formula of the first vows in the Society. It impresses us with the solemnity of the occasion, and the thought of the great inter-cession for us lends us hope and courage. Our prayer is to understand thoroughly the many great benefits which we have received from God, that by grateful remembrance of them we may attain to perfect love and service. Thus at the end of the retreat we find ourselves at the same point whence we started, the perfect service of

God. In the second meditation of the first day
we set before ourselves the knowledge, love and
service of our Creator. Yet we deliberately
considered it from an inadequate point of view
in order to work up little by little to a full
understanding and practice of it. We looked at
it, so to speak, from a philosophical standpoint
endeavouring to convince ourselves of what mere
reason had to tell us, and without as yet laying
much emphasis on the love, but rather on service,
our sheer duty. Now, however, we have contemplated not merely our abstract duty, so to
call it, but also how we have failed to fulfil it,
and what punishment we have deserved; how
Our Blessed Lord has come to save us, how
He has given us an example and has died for
us, and by rising again has manifested the bliss
and glory which He designs for us. And all
the while we have been stirring ourselves up to
more generous consecration of ourselves, to more
utter sacrifice. Now, therefore, to crown all, we
are to see that the love of God alone matters,
that it is our most divine privilege, as it must
be our supreme desire, to possess it as fully as
we may.

GOD'S BENEFITS. We begin by considering
God's benefits in themselves, what He has done
for us and what He has given us. It is not
new gifts of God, hitherto unthought of, that
we need to discover, but rather we must aim

at a more perfect understanding of benefits which have been long familiar to us by name. We may follow the usual division: benefits received in common with others, and benefits peculiar to ourselves. That we came into being at all was a great gift of God: that we have been created, as we saw at the outset of the retreat, with a definite end, the noblest of all ends, comprising within itself our own complete happiness: that we have been given all the helps we need, and much more than we need, towards the attainment of that end: that Christ came to redeem us from original sin and actual sins, and to put us again in the way of obtaining that end: that He left with us the sacrament of His Body and Blood — in considering all this and much besides we are repeating, from a slightly different standpoint, a great part of our retreat. And we think of more personal favours, that we were born in the true fold, that we received a Catholic education and a call to religious life, that graces and blessings have freely been showered upon us, in spite of much faithlessness. Or it may be that we were outside the Church, and were sweetly led into it. But in any case the supreme mercy shown us is surely this, that at the present moment we stand before God, eager to offer Him entire surrender and uttermost abandonment, surrounded by every possible means of making that offer effective, and inflamed thereto by God's own urging. God has ever been beforehand with us, helping us with His grace and external providence, in spite of our kicking against the goad; we feel that it is so still, that He is lavishing blessings upon us, indeed, that, so far as is possible, it is Himself that He is endeavouring to communicate more and more to us, in all that He does to draw us close to Himself, in the Holy Eucharist, in the transforming influence of His grace, which makes us, as St. Peter says (II Pet. I, 4), sharers in the Divine Nature, exalting the whole being of the soul to a superhuman life and activity, fastening intellect and will upon Himself as our supernatural end. We in our turn, to make as generous an answer as possible to our Divine Lover, beg Him to take for His very own ourselves and all that is in any ways ours to give Him, and we use the formula of oblation which is the matter of the third point of this contemplation.

GOD'S PRESENCE, POWER AND ESSENCE. God, according to St. Thomas (*Summa* I, q. 8, a. 3), is everywhere by His presence, power and essence. This truth we proceed to apply to the matter in hand; having considered God's benefits in themselves, we consider how He does not confer them from a distance, but how He is present to them, and, as it were, working in them. Finally we reflect that they are but a faint reflection of His own infinite perfection.

We may think of the Incarnation, of the Holy Eucharist, of the Christ's Mystical Body the Church, as a fulfilment of God's desire to be present to us and communicate Himself to us. Then we may reflect upon the things about us — hill and vale and sea, the lilies of the field, the varied beauty of the animal world; it is only God's sustaining and permeating presence that encircles us with the galaxy of His handiwork, and where we behold the excellence of His creatures, there we must learn to behold our Heavenly Father, winning us by the display of His own excellence and of His tender Providence. We may use them or no, according to the requirements of His service; but the sublimest of all uses is, after all, sheer contemplation. Nor must we exclude the handiwork of man from our thoughts; it is from God no less than from man. Nay, our fellow-men, needless to say, are utterly from God also, so far as there is anything good in them, body or soul. But the crowning gift is that of grace, our deification, as the Fathers and St. Thomas himself called it, the raising of our soul to a state and activity so far exceeding the possibilities of mere nature as to be called by Holy Writ, as we have seen (II Pet. I, 4), a sharing of the Divine Nature. So, then, we conclude with God not merely presenting Himself to us from without, but penetrating and transforming the innermost nature of our soul, out of His communicative love. His presence in creatures should always lead us up to His presence in our own souls, a most important thought in the spiritual life. Once more we make the offering to be given below; but we may refer it more especially to the thoughts before us, increasing our sense of God's presence in ourselves and elsewhere, in all places loving and adoring Him.

But then we come to think of God exerting His power in our behalf. Again we may adopt the triple division roughly followed when speaking of God's presence: we may think of His activity in the Incarnation and all that belongs to it, of His activity in all creatures, living and inanimate, including man: and most of all of His working in ourselves by His grace, thinking perhaps rather of actual than of sanctifying grace. God has thought out, if we may use such human language, our whole course, and provided amply for our every need, and even for our every failing: and always with one object, to unite us more closely to Himself. And again we make the return of utter self-abandonment.

And now, in a supreme effort, we endeavour to think of God, not explicitly as good to us, but as good in Himself. We have to rise from creatures to Him, to realise that whatever perfection we can detect in things created, that perfection is contained in God also, but without any limitation or least defect. Whatever power or love or holiness we see in others is only a far-off image and participation of that boundless sea of power and love and holiness which is God. Creation is so beautiful that it needs all our efforts not to lose our hearts to creatures; how much more the Creator! For a brief space we think of God in this way, as best our poor nature can, forming our idea of Him, as we necessarily must, by taking what perfection we know and denying it any limit. Even as the artist has trained himself to recognise the full perfection of created beauty, so we apply ourselves to the sovereign perfection of God; and thus we understand a little better that there is only one being worth admiration, worth understanding, worth loving, worth entire devotion. Such devotion alone can be the adequate fruit of contemplating Him, when we are moved, not by any profit to accrue to ourselves, but by the immeasurable desert of God Himself. Supreme charity is to love God because He is God.

THE PRAYER. 'Take, O Lord, and receive all my liberty, my memory, my understanding, and all my will, all that I have and possess; Thou hast given me all these things, to thee, O Lord, I restore them: all are thine, dispose of them wholly according to Thy will. Give me thy love and thy grace, for this is enough for me.'

Such is St. Ignatius' prayer. It is easy to see its purpose and spirit, but not easy to adopt it and make it entirely one's own. For it means the entire absence or breaking down of any the least barrier or reserve that can come between us and God. Every time we repeat it we may ponder it afresh, and hope to enter into it more and more. It will also be profitable to renew the offering of ourselves contained in our vows.

Printed by HERDER & Co., Freiburg im Breisgau (Germany).